PRE-ISLAMIC CARPETS AND TEXTILES
FROM EASTERN LANDS

PRE-ISLAMIC CARPETS AND TEXTILES FROM EASTERN LANDS

FRIEDRICH SPUHLER

Dar al-Athar al-Islamiyyah   The al-Sabah Collection, Kuwait

Thames & Hudson

First published in the United Kingdom in 2014
by Thames & Hudson Ltd, 181A High Holborn, London WC1V 7QX

First paperback edition

Collection series editor
Salam Kaoukji

Photography and photo-editing
Muhammad Ali

Assisted by
Robert Lorenzo
Michael Tejero

Design by Maggi Smith

British Library Cataloguing-in-Publication Data
A catalogue record for this book is available from the British Library

ISBN 978-0-500-97055-3

Printed and bound in China by C&C Offset Printing Co. Ltd

CONTENTS

FOREWORD

by Sheikh Nasser Sabah al-Ahmad al-Sabah

In the decades that followed the acquisition of my first objects in 1975, The al-Sabah Collection has grown dramatically. In addition to art from the Islamic world, it now includes a significant number of pre-Islamic objects, dating from the 4th millennium BCE to the dawn of Islam. While metal objects tend to dominate this aspect of the collection, there is also a notable assembly of carpet fragments from the 3rd to the 7th centuries CE.

Under the leadership of my wife, Hussah Sabah al-Salem al-Sabah, director-general of the Dar al-Athar al-Islamiyyah and co-owner of The al-Sabah Collection, we are now able to connect with wider audiences from the Islamic world and beyond through travelling exhibitions and loans, archaeological excavations, educational activities for children and adults, participation in digital collections and the publication of scholarly books.

2012 saw the publication of *Carpets from Islamic Lands* by Friedrich Spuhler. This book focused on carpets from the Islamic period in The al-Sabah Collection. The present volume, *Pre-Islamic Carpets and Textiles from Eastern Lands*, also by Dr Spuhler, continues to explore carpets in the collection, looking at those created in the four hundred years between the 3rd and the 7th centuries CE. Little has been published about pile carpets from this period, but just as the art of the carpets feeds my own passion for them, learning about and discovering their history and manufacturing techniques nourishes Dr Spuhler's.

It is our hope that the publication of this book, which includes many pieces that have never been published before, will reach and inspire readers: those who recognize themselves in the history; those exploring the art of ages past and those who have objects and ideas to add to the body of knowledge. We also hope that it will provide the missing link between the "Pazyryk" carpet, dating from *c.* 400 BCE and found almost intact in a frozen tomb in the Altai region, and the 13th-century Konya fragments. Finally while the names of the artists who designed and wove these carpets have been lost, it is our hope that through this book an appreciation for their artistry may be perpetuated.

ACKNOWLEDGMENTS

Many of the acknowledgments that appeared in the earlier volume *Carpets from Islamic Lands* (2012) could be republished here. But gratitude and appreciation should be repeated!

I remember my first meeting with Sheikh Nasser al-Sabah during a tour of the Museum für Islamische Kunst in Berlin, when he unexpectedly asked whether I would be interested in writing a catalogue of the carpets in his collection. I immediately said yes, without any idea of the surprises that were awaiting me in Kuwait. His initiative was later energetically supported by Sheikha Hussah, and I continue to owe my very deepest thanks to both of them.

When one experiences an exciting find with a colleague, it creates a sense of shared guardianship. This often blossoms into friendship, of the kind that Julia and I share with Salam (Sue) Kaoukji, who thoughtfully and meticulously edited my catalogues.

In the case of the pre-Islamic fragments, which were the true surprise of the al-Sabah carpet collection, a kind of protective circle was formed around a shared secret. These fragile pieces required special care from all the hands through which they passed. From the conservation department, Sophie Budden, assisted by Benjamin Hilario and Honorio (Rally) Lim, made sure that all the objects that had to be transported to London were well secured. There, the carpet fragments were professionally cleaned and restored by Louise Squire.

I am also grateful to Manuel Keene and Deborah Freeman for their continuous support and valuable contributions.

In recent years, photography has played an ever more crucial role in the presentation of art books, and has helped create an intimate relationship between the viewer and the object. In comparison with the relatively unwieldy medium of words, which the author must rely upon, the photographer speaks more directly to the reader. The photographer, Mohammed Ali, assisted by Robert Lorenzo, carried out this task admirably. Juanna Fernandes and Marsha Sequeira have handled all the arrangements of our visits very smoothly and resolved every detail efficiently, always with good humour.

In London, Katie Marsh wove all the visible and invisible threads of this project together, patiently and quietly – at least on the phone – and the team from Thames & Hudson, especially Flora Spiegel, handled all matters related to the publication resourcefully.

And last but not least we would like to thank Dr Fabrizio Lombardi, and his wife Dr Maria Cristina Gianni, Milan, who kindly offered to photograph the wall paintings of Afrasiab so they could be reproduced in this publication.

My warmest thanks go to my wife, Julia Plato. Without her, this book would not exist.

Friedrich Spuhler

Detail, Cat 1.10 (LNS 63 R)

INTRODUCTION

A selection of pre-Islamic carpet fragments preserved in the al-Sabah Collection was featured in *Carpets from Islamic Lands*.[1] To have these objects tangibly in front of me was a defining experience of my more than forty-year involvement with oriental rugs; my teacher Kurt Erdmann had long dreamed of a similar moment, but waited in vain for a lifetime! The days that followed this first viewing were exciting and often hectic as we attempted to divide these unique pieces into groups, and where possible, to match up fragments based on their edges. The results of this process are discussed in the first section of this catalogue, but it can be said in advance that the three carpets whose dimensions can be reconstructed are small in format and a maximum of 2.5 metres in length. They are therefore very different from the legendary "Spring of Khosrau", a carpet taken as booty by soldiers during the conquest of the palace of Ctesiphon (south of modern-day Baghdad) in CE 637, and which, according to early written sources, is reputed to have reached the fantastical size of 600 m².

The al-Sabah examples speak a different language that has no connection with the splendour and magnificence of the Sasanian court. Village-dwellers and nomads needed coverings for the ground to give protection from the cold and damp; thus, the crude knots incorporating shag on the reverse served to provide increased insulation. Decorative themes included familiar animals and the hunt, but unfortunately the coarse finish did not allow for any subtleties of style or representation. Mythological scenes – with the exception of the examples representing winged dragons – hardly feature, but considering the general style and iconography adopted by the weavers, these carpets are nonetheless quite impressive.

Although this collection of carpet fragments and the three reconstructed small-format rugs is remarkable, its range of subject matter is not extensive enough to allow the carpets to be grouped based on stylistic characteristics. Minor technical differences have also proved to be too arbitrary for this purpose, but fortunately the Carbon-14 dating of each piece has afforded us with a chronological sequence.[2]

The second section of this book is devoted to silk produced in territories under Sasanian and Sogdian rule. In the Middle Ages such textiles were occasionally brought to Europe, where they were used as coverings for relics, and survived well-protected in church treasuries.[3] Consequently, these textiles were given a prominent place in the first illustrated publications on the history of textile art, such as those that were published in the late nineteenth and early twentieth centuries by the German art historian Julius Lessing.[4] They owe their incorporation into art history to famed rock reliefs, such as the Sasanian representations at Taq-i Bustan in southern Persia, the wall paintings of Dunhuang, Panjikent and Afrasiab, and not least to the predominantly Russian excavations that brought to light Sasanian representations on silver vessels (see pp. 18–19). A more recent wave of Sasanian-period and Sogdian textiles has reached the West since the turn of the twenty-first century. Likely sources for these are Tibetan monasteries and the many burial sites along the Silk Road, such as Astana, near Turfan.

The range of samite textiles offers a different picture than the carpets: here we chose to divide the examples into variants featuring birds, mammals and mythological creatures, particularly since I still – albeit hypothetically – maintain that the different animal motifs used to decorate garments had a direct connection to the rank or profession of their wearer.

PART I

CARPETS FROM THE SASANIAN PERIOD

Although the Sasanian-period carpet fragments in The al-Sabah Collection have fundamentally changed our understanding of the history of oriental rugs, the earliest phases of this history still contain substantial gaps of several centuries for which no examples have yet been discovered. Furthermore, the episode in the history of carpets under consideration here begins abruptly and does not follow the artistic tradition of the so-called "Pazyryk" carpet: the ancestor of carpets that stands at the beginning of the chronology. The Pazyryk carpet (Fig. 1.1) was found in 1949 in a Scythian burial mound in the Altai Mountains, but regrettably there is no reliable evidence that allows us to ascertain whether it was brought from far away as a gift to the buried ruler, or if it was made in the immediate vicinity of the place it was found.[1]

Clearly, the technically sophisticated knotted Pazyryk carpet with 3,600 knots per dm^2 must have had precursors, and one can only hope that future discoveries will uncover material that sheds some light on how and where these precursors originated. The Pazyryk carpet's complex design, with its two animal frieze borders proceeding in opposite directions accompanied by guard stripes, would not have been conceivable without a lengthy period of development. The inner frieze includes a procession of deer, while the outer frieze features men on horseback and others leading horses whose saddlecloths are decorated with different designs. The relatively small central field is divided into a chequerboard of starburst vegetal motifs of a style that is difficult to classify. Some authors, among them Volkmar Gantzhorn, believe it is of Achaemenid derivation.[2]

Because the Pazyryk carpet is followed by a gap of around 700 years for which virtually no examples exist, it is difficult to speak of it as part of a tradition. The basic principles of the

borders around all four sides and the field divided into squares remained a topos of Sasanian-period carpets. As mentioned above, its technique is so sophisticated that continuous development must be ruled out for the Sasanian-period examples presented here.

A few carpet fragments dating from the third to fourth century CE (Fig. 1.2) were discovered in Dunhuang and Loulan, in western China, by Sir Aurel Stein, but they are so small in size that their designs are almost impossible to reconstruct.[3] Furthermore, there is no transition between these fragments and the next known stage of carpet development, the Anatolian animal carpets of the thirteenth century.

A group of some two dozen fragments has now assisted in bridging the gap between these scattered examples. These fragments, now in The al-Sabah Collection, can be described as the most sensational discovery in the recent history of pile carpets, especially since they include examples by means of which the dimensions of the original carpets can be

Fig. 1.1 *opposite*
Detail, fragment of the "Pazyryk Carpet", State Hermitage Museum, St Petersburg, Inv. no. 1687/93 (detail). Pile carpet, wool, knot technique, 183 x 200 cm, Pazyryk Culture, 5th–4th century BCE, Pazyryk Barrow No. 5 (excavations by S. I. Rudenko, 1949), Altai Region, Pazyryk Boundary, valley of the river Bolshoy Ulagan, Russia. © The State Hermitage Museum, St Petersburg/Photo by Vladimir Terebenin, Leonard Kheifets and Yuri Molodkovets.

Fig. 1.2 *above*
Carpet fragment from Loulan
British Museum, Inv. no. MAS.693.
© The Trustees of the British Museum.

Figs 1.3, 1.4, 1.5, 1.6
Details showing the shag on the backs
of rug fragments.

reconstructed, as, for example, with Cat. 1.1, Cat. 1.9, and Cat. 1.13. It is likewise worthy of note that neither Kurt Erdmann nor Arthur Upham Pope and Phyllis Ackerman had any doubts that knotted pile carpets from the Sasanian era must have existed.[4]

In the individual descriptions, I thought it necessary to list the properties common to each group, such as alleged place of discovery, and materials and techniques, including ply, spin, colour, knots and treatment of edges. The focus on knots allows readers to get a sense of the feel and texture of these previously unknown types of carpets, and the descriptions make it possible to identify individual details that are specific to each group, and perhaps interpret the independent features of the iconography.

The Sasanian-period carpet fragments are surprisingly coarse in texture. A single wool yarn can be up to 2.5 mm thick and is always Z-spun. All the carpets feature two or more colours, worked in asymmetrical knots (Fig. 1.3). The warp and weft are made up of similar wool, with the warp often consisting of yarn in two colours – light and dark brown – which are Z-spun and S-plied (Fig. 1.4). Because each knot is made up of two thick woollen yarns, the resulting knot count is low, at around 400 knots per dm². Following a series of three to

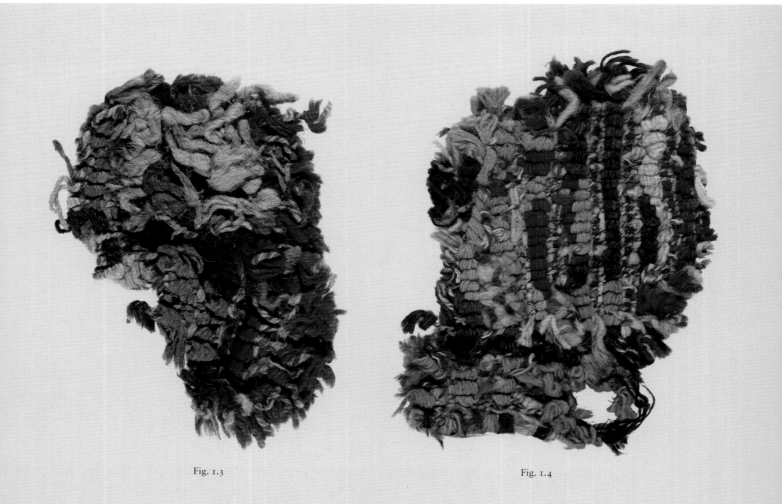

Fig. 1.3

Fig. 1.4

five rows of knots, an additional "row" is added on the reverse. These are composed of different materials: the yarn used for knots, unspun tufts of wool of considerable thickness, and even strips of leather between 2 and 5 mm wide are combined with felted material in order to provide insulation from the cold ground (Fig. 1.5). This unusual thickness of 2–3 cm clearly makes sense if the carpet was intended for use inside a tent or a cave. The thickness creates a "blurring" of the design, which is exacerbated by the fact that the number of yarns in each knot varies. On the whole the warp is formed by a white and a dark yarn twisted together. The weft shoots are thick and form a slightly flexible layer, within which the warp, unlike that of later pile carpets, must perform a slight twisting movement.

The colours of the wool pile are fresh and lively and include three shades of red, two shades of blue (indigo), a bright apple-green and a pale yellow, as well as an undyed white and also an undyed brownish shade of black. Furthermore, the finishing of the sides displays an unusual feature that does not appear in later pile carpets, in which one is accustomed to seeing the warp yarns emerging as fringes from the pile surface of a carpet's narrow ends. This group also features applied fringes on the long sides, in an alternating double yarn of white

Fig. 1.5

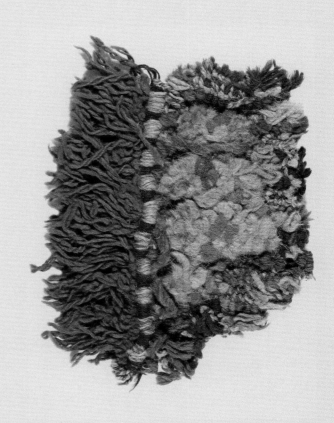

Fig. 1.6

Fig. 1.7
Mural from Panjikent with merchants drinking, State Hermitage Museum,
St Petersburg, Inv. no. B-2703. © The State Hermitage Museum, St Petersburg/
Photo by Vladimir Terebenin, Leonard Kheifets and Yuri Molodkovets.

and brown, that were stitched to the sides after the weaving was completed (Fig. 1.6). The carefree irregularity, predominantly created by the knots and the weft, results in carpets that are coarse in both design and texture, reflecting their foremost function as a warm and protective ground-covering, rather than as works of textile art. They would undoubtedly have been items of everyday use for peasant or possibly nomadic households, but

so far as use by nomadic peoples is concerned, these rugs were no better-suited to transportation than were felts, because they must have been extremely difficult to roll.

These carpet fragments entered the Collection in around 1997, and originate exclusively from northern Afghanistan. Dealers consistently give the province of Samangan as the place of discovery, and the cave of Ayr Malik in the village of

Duab-i Shahpesand is often mentioned.[5] The reliability of this information remains open to question, but the regular recurrence of this provenance over the years means that it certainly cannot be excluded. This province of present-day Afghanistan was part of the great Persian Empire and remained so through to the reign of the Timurids (CE 1370–1507). The carpets and textiles were allegedly recovered in various inhabitable caves that were found along the Silk Road and were sometimes used as places of refuge as well as burial, including the aforementioned cave of Ayr Malik.[6] Usually positioned high up in the rock walls, these caves could only be reached by climbing.

Before we catalogue individual examples, it should be reaffirmed that the material is not sufficient to allow a division into groups on stylistic grounds. Instead, the examples have been

Fig. 1.8
Sasanian silver dish depicting a king seated on a carpet, diameter 25.7 cm,
State Hermitage, St Petersburg, Inv. no. S-4. © The State Hermitage Museum, St Petersburg/
Photo by Vladimir Terebenin, Leonard Kheifets and Yuri Molodkovets.

Fig. 1.9
Sasanian silver dish depicting a king reclining on a couch with musicians, diameter 23.2 cm, State Hermitage Museum, St Petersburg, inv no. S.47. © The State Hermitage Museum, St Petersburg/ Photo by Vladimir Terebenin, Leonard Kheifets and Yuri Molodkovets.

divided into three groups according to their age, as established by the results of radiocarbon dating (Carbon-14). These tests were carried out at different institutions and at different points in time.[7]

DEPICTIONS OF SASANIAN CARPETS

Sasanian and Sogdian wall paintings document a great many more robes and other general-purpose textiles than they do carpets. Even when floor coverings are represented in the murals of Panjikent (Fig. 1.7), the artist may well have resorted to depicting textile designs;[8] consequently, there is little connection with real carpets.[9] In Sasanian reliefs, a wide range of textiles is also represented, but pile carpets and flatweaves are almost totally absent.

A more useful source of comparison, however, can be found in Sasanian metalwork. Silver dishes often feature throne scenes, and a carpet would invariably be placed beneath the throne in the Iranian and eastern regions of the Islamic world. In the later Islamic period, this symbiosis between carpet and throne survived, and during the Safavid era, which was the golden age of the court carpet, it could even be said that the

carpet and its medallion marked the position of the throne.

One outstanding reproduction of a Sasanian carpet appears on a silver dish in the State Hermitage Museum, St Petersburg (Fig. 1.8).[10] The scene depicts a king seated cross-legged on a carpet and characteristically holding a cup between his thumb and forefinger: a standard scene in royal iconography. A distinction between the field of the carpet and its scrolling vine border is clearly visible. The central field is almost entirely filled by a bold and nearly symmetrical motif of lotus blooms. Beneath the king's left knee another floral element appears, this time in the form of an unfurling bud. The individuated, slightly curved vegetal motifs on the opposite side are similar to those in our border fragments (Cat. 1.6 and Cat. 1.7); however, there are no carpets with vegetal decoration of this kind among our examples. An explanation for this absence will be sought in the text that follows.

The king rests his right elbow on two rounded cushions decorated with simple geometric motifs, which invite a comparison with the "flatweave" cushion (Cat. 1.17). Similar cushions can be seen in other depictions of princely figures reclining on day-beds or couches (Fig. 1.9).[11]

Cat. 1.1 A PROCESSION OF STAGS
Eastern Iran, 2nd–4th century CE

Fragment a: length 141.5 cm, width 62 cm
Fragment b: length 56.5 cm, width 40 cm
Fragment c: length 38 cm, width 26 cm
Fragment d: length 91.5 cm, width 25 cm

Reconstructed
length: 192 cm, width 118 cm
Warp: wool, white and brown (goat's hair?) z2s, very thick yarn
Weft: wool, white and red, 4–6 zx2, very thick yarn
Knots: wool, z, 2–4 threads, asymmetrical, V 25, H 12

Height of pile: 1–1.5 cm
Back: 4–6 cm apart (irregularly spaced) rows of yarn and unspun wool or goat's hair, as well as strips of felt and goatskin in U-shaped loops.

C-14 dating of
fragment "a": Zürich, CE 140 ± 50; Oxford, CE 225 ± 40
Provenance: reportedly from Samangan Province, northern Afghanistan

Inv. no. LNS 47 R a–d

By joining the four remaining fragments of this carpet one can estimate its original dimensions as having been: 192 × 118 (or 111) cm.

Fragment "a" clearly shows the motif that takes up the main field, as well as a section of the narrow end border. Successions of alternating red and bluish-grey animals in striding posture are arranged facing in the same direction. Their hooves are cloven and their antlers, which are easy to overlook, appear to be thrust out in front of them, indicating that these definitely represent stags.

The antlers rise vertically in relation to the body, suggesting that the stags might be grazing, an impression strengthened by their open mouths. The position of the head could also be interpreted as an attacking pose, although I think that is unlikely here. This type of posture is well known from woven wool braids decorated with grotesque animals that were once used to decorate women's skirts. The Abegg Foundation in Riggisberg, Switzerland, devoted a special exhibition to these "fabulous creatures from the desert sands" in 2001.[12]

Detail, Cat. 1.1 (LNS 47 R), fragment b (above); fragment a (opposite)

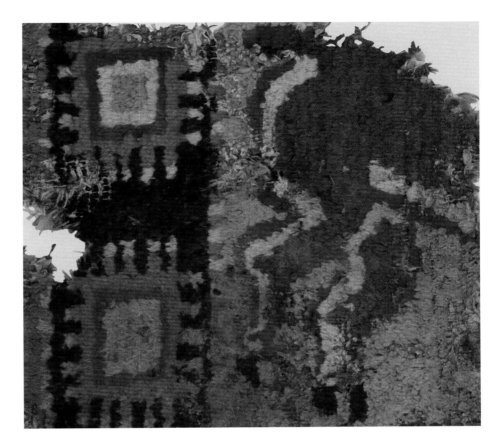

Fragment "b" is much smaller and depicts two motifs from the narrow end border that include an animal, or rather its bluish-grey hindquarters with a very pronounced purple abrash (the effect produced by the uneven tones of different lots of dyed yarn) towards the front. The animal's head is missing, but fortunately survives on the outermost edge of fragment "a" in the form of a bluish-grey neck and head outlined in red. This enables us to say with certainty that the two fragments were once connected, and consequently allows us to establish the original warp length.

The small section of the field contained in fragment "c" includes most of two forelegs and part of a head, which in all probability represents the last animal in the bottom row. Several flowers indicate that the yellow ground of the field was decorated with scattered floral motifs.

Fragment "d" depicts a section from the border, whose survival can be viewed as a particular stroke of good fortune because it completes our picture of this truly remarkable compartment carpet. The tassel in the lower right-hand corner is unusual, and may have served to tie the carpet in place. The outer guard stripe that forms the carpet's edge comprises a red-and-yellow chequered pattern, and the inner guard stripe features the familiar "dice" pattern on a dark brown ground with a minor red-and-white striped band and a bluish-green line along one of its edges. A denticulate red-and-white band provides the frame for the compartments and at the same time serves as a kind of base for the stag motifs.

The "primitive" style, the glowing colours of the animals, and the naivety with which they are depicted all point to this being the product of a nomadic society. It would therefore be pointless to seek out literary sources or any centre where such carpets might have been woven. They were produced for personal use and for the pleasure of the weavers, and it is highly unlikely that they would have been considered tradable goods. As local products they would not have travelled far, and were therefore almost certainly woven somewhere in the vicinity of the place of discovery. The crude nature of the rendering can in some cases be compared to the style of certain hunting and animal scenes shown on silver vessels.

It might appear as though our description of this early piece has become somewhat overcrowded with details. However, when we describe classical pile carpets such as those made under the Mamluks, Ottomans, Safavids and Mughals we have over a century of research to help us identify the essential features relating to compartments and borders. On the other hand, with Sasanian carpets the few extant examples are still unfamiliar territory, and art historians have a great many gaps to fill. Detailed observations are therefore necessary if we are to understand concepts such as the elements that might be specific to each group. Peculiarities of technique can help to achieve an initial consensus, as can the use of dyes and the choice of colour.

Detail, Cat. 1.1 (LNS 47 R), fragment a

Cat. 1.2 BORDER FRAGMENTS
WITH DETAIL OF FIELD
Eastern Iran, 2nd–4th century CE

Fragment e: length 37 cm, width 26.5 cm
(main piece in the group)
Fragment f: length 8.5 cm, width 8 cm
Fragment g: length 19.5 cm, width 17 cm
Warp: wool, white, Z2S
Weft: wool, Z3; 2x
Knots: wool, Z, 2–4 threads, asymmetrical,
V 18, H 16
Back: unspun felted wool, attached
horizontally, mainly every three
rows of knots; no knots on the back
of the selvedge under the outer
guard stripe
Provenance: reportedly from Samangan Province,
northern Afghanistan

Inv. no. LNS 47 R e–g

Despite its narrow width of just under 27 cm, fragment "e", the largest fragment of this group, includes the main design elements of the original carpet.

A border of foliate scrolls meanders on a white ground, wherein each individual leaf is rendered in two colours, such as yellow and red, or blue and ochre, that serve to distinguish the inner from the outer contour of the leaf. In the outer edging stripe one can see a pattern of repeated square-shaped compartments enclosing rectilinear quatrefoils somewhat related to the inner guard stripe of the previous carpet. A continuous red line edges the border on both sides.

A small portion of the inner field is still preserved and features staggered rows of brown squares. The same motif can be seen on fragment "g", demonstrating that it was once part of the same field. We do not know, however, whether the entire field was patterned in this way, and as the few carpets and floor coverings depicted on Sasanian silverware do not feature centralized medallions, I am inclined to assume that the spots would have been an all-over motif, perhaps representing leopard skin.

Fragment "f" is scarcely wider than a human hand, and was originally part of the outer edging stripe. With a little imagination a quatrefoil can be discerned inside the rectangle. Of particular interest is a tiny piece of selvedge that consists of a light-coloured overcast warp bundle. This form of edge finish evidently goes back to the early Sasanian period and is still in use today.

To judge by the proportions of the surviving border, the carpet must have been small in format. I would estimate that it was around 150 to 180 cm long and a maximum of 100 cm wide.

Cat. 1.3 SMALL BORDER FRAGMENT
Eastern Iran, 2nd–4th century CE

Length: 16.5 cm, width 18 cm
Warp: wool, white, Z2S, wavy
Weft: wool, white, Z4, two-ply inserted
straight
Knots: wool, Z3, asymmetrical, V 30, H 10
Selvedge: warp overcast with wool, Z,
reddish-brown and ochre in
U-shaped, open loops
Back: thick brown and white unspun wool
inserted in rows, usually every four
rows of knots
Provenance: reportedly from Samangan Province,
northern Afghanistan

Inv. no. LNS 47 R h

This border fragment is so small that one can only make a very vague attempt at describing the decoration.

The outer band could represent part of a reciprocal scrolling vine on a red ground, and the light-coloured band that separates the guard stripe from the main band is unfortunately too fragmentary for one even to attempt a description of it, although one could speculate that the dark lines are part of a leafy arabesque.

More interesting than such speculations about the design, however, is a technical detail: on the long side, fringes of reddish-brown and ochre-coloured wool have been applied to the selvedge. This detail demonstrates that carpets with fringes on all sides already existed at that time.

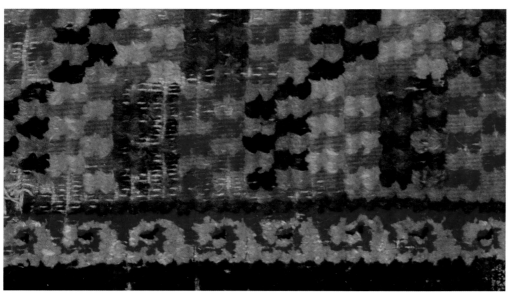

Cat. 1.4 "MOSAIC" BORDER FRAGMENT
Eastern Iran, 2nd–4th century CE

Length: 114 cm, width 33 cm
Warp: wool, white, z3s, wavy, fine
Weft: wool, very fine, 4–5 z or 2–3 z, then row of knots
Knots: wool, 3–4z, pile height 0.5 cm, v 28, h 16
Back: wool, light-coloured and brown, thick brown goat's hair and woven fabric, the latter in plain weave
C-14 dating: Oxford, CE 157 ± 28
Provenance: reportedly from Maimana, Faryab Province, northern Afghanistan

Inv. no. LNS 64 R

This, in my opinion, is one of the most attractive Sasanian fragments in The al-Sabah Collection, with its seemingly unique style of decoration that differs fundamentally from that of the "animal carpets".

The marked contrast between the unpatterned dark brown ground and the brightly coloured border, which likewise differs from the more commonly used borders of foliate scrolls, creates a striking effect. Although one cannot be absolutely sure that the entire field was plain – in theory, there could have been a lozenge or square in the centre – this seems unlikely since none of the carpets from this period feature centralized motifs.

The border design is subtly laid out and coloured with staggered rows of chequered rectangles in tones of blue, orange, green and red. Each rectangle is divided into paired rows of squares in two shades of the same colour. This gives rise to a mosaic-like pattern, which probably derived from mosaic floors. Patterns such as this may well have originated in Syrian regions or Roman-ruled Byzantium.

Between the border and the field is a red "wave-scroll" guard stripe, punctuated with blue against an off-white ground, and separated from the border by a blue line.

**Cat. 1.5 FRAGMENT OF BORDER
WITH SECTION OF FIELD**
Eastern Iran, 3rd–4th century CE

Length: 24.5 cm, width 25 cm
Warp: wool, white and brown, Z2S, wavy
Weft: wool, white and brown, Z2
and 3 double and inserted straight
Knots: wool, Z3, asymmetrical, V 42, H 25
Back: wool or goat's hair, thick yarn
inserted horizontally every four rows
of knots
C-14 dating: Oxford, CE 218 ± 27
Provenance: reportedly from Samangan Province,
northern Afghanistan

Inv. no. LNS 53 R

Thanks to the surviving section of its border, this carpet can be linked with the carpet depicting stags from a royal hunt (Cat. 1.13) that features a border of reciprocal light and dark stepped crenellations and a "wave-scroll" motif.

It is likely that the soil composition of the place in which this fragment was buried was such that all the colours have now faded away. The field decoration was probably once set against a red ground, and the few dark lines that remain may well have served to outline the different fields of colour that are no longer distinguishable.

Since we have no other examples of purely linear patterns, we will refrain from attempting to interpret the zigzag line and curves that might represent anything from the leg or neck of a figure, or maybe even a harpy. The wool has also lost most of its sheen and is very fragile.

**Cat. 1.6 FOLIATE BORDER
FRAGMENT
Eastern Iran, 4th–6th century CE**

Length: 88 cm, width 29 cm
Warp: wool, white and brown, z2s, wavy
Weft: wool, white, z2, two-ply straight
Knots: wool, z, three- and four-ply,
asymmetrical, V 13, H 14
Back: Brown goat's hair and white unspun
wool in rows, every three rows of
knots
C-14 dating: Zürich, CE 350 ± 50

Inv. no. LNS 51 R

The lobed foliate motifs of this luxuriant split-leaf scroll are enhanced with red alternately outlined with blue and ochre that cause the leaves to resemble flower calyxes. A continuous red border traces the outer contour of the scroll whereas an off-white border lines its inner contour. In addition, the background of the border is divided by the scroll into blue on the outer edge and dark brown on the inner edge. "Wave-scroll" motifs form the guard stripes – in red against off-white on the field side, and in brown punctuated with red against off-white on the outer edge. Unfortunately, what remains of the field is so small that nothing of its pattern is preserved, aside from parts of one blue and two red dots.

Cat. 1.7 A PROCESSION OF MYTHICAL CREATURES
Eastern Iran, 4th–6th century CE

Length: 98 cm, width 86 cm
Warp: wool, white and brown, z2s, wavy
Weft: wool, z, predominantly two-ply, but also three-ply
Knots: wool, z2+3, asymmetrical, also some offset knots, V 27, H 25
Back: white unspun wool, occasionally also brown, z, every seven or more rarely eight rows, thickness 4 mm
C-14 dating: Kiel, CE 310 ± 30
Provenance: reportedly from Samangan Province, northern Afghanistan

Inv. no. LNS 73 R

Both this carpet fragment, which has been carbon dated to the first half of the fourth century CE, as well as the strikingly similar fragment (Cat. 1.8) carbon dated to a slightly earlier period, originated, as most of the Sasanian fragments in the Collection, from the caves of Samangan, in northern Afghanistan.

A procession of fantastical creatures, the likes of which can be traced to ancient Near Eastern art,[13] fills the field of this long-format carpet bordered on its two longer sides with a foliate scroll border of a type that was obviously very popular in the area (see, for example, the scroll borders of Cat. 1.6, 1.9 and 1.16).

The central animal with its distinctive green pelt outlined in red, yellow and black is fortunately fully preserved and points to a hybrid of dragon and leogryph. The creature's threatening head is rendered in an eye-catching blue; its dragon-like curling snout is opened wide, baring menacing teeth; and its short, pointed ears jut forward. The curved neck is outlined with a short, curly mane, and the large wing is detailed with a chequered panel, typical of Sasanian iconography, and virtually identical to the shoulder or wing panels depicted on some of the early textiles in the Collection (Cat. 2.10, 2.11 and 2.14).[14]

The adjacent creature with its spotted, yellowish body is difficult to identify as it is only partially preserved, although the spotted pelt might point to a leopard. A single paw from the third animal can be seen close to the hindquarters of the central creature.

The lobed leaves of the border scroll are set against a blue ground outlined in off-white and detailed with red, green and brown, and chequered triangle-shaped motifs fill the intervening areas. The inner guard stripes are decorated with a red "wave-scroll" motif punctuated with blue against a white ground, and the outer stripe with rosettes of varying colours, closely related to the rosettes on the border fragment (Cat. 1.2).

In "animal carpets" from this area, one usually finds animals that nomads would have been familiar with in their daily lives, and, although it seems unlikely that they had access to the subject of mythical animals from early silver vessels[15] or silk textiles (see, for example, Cat. 2.8, pp. 120–21), they must have been knowledgeable about the subject through encounters garnered on the various Silk Roads.

Detail of central winged animal, Cat. 1.7 (LNS 73 R)

Detail of border scroll, Cat. 1.7 (LNS 73 R)

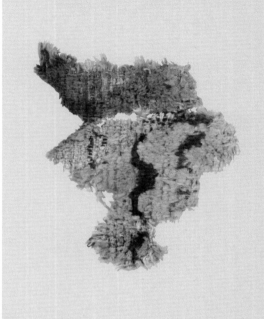

Cat. 1.8 A SINGLE MYTHICAL CREATURE
Eastern Iran, 4th–6th century CE

Length: 93 cm, width 107 cm
Warp: wool, white, occasionally brown, Z2S, wavy
Weft: wool, Z2, untwisted
Knots: wool, Z2+3, asymmetrical, also some offset knots, V 26, H 22
Selvedge: red wool, with remains of applied red fringes sewn to the long sides
Back: unspun wool, white and occasionally brown, loose Z, inserted every eight rows, thickness 4–4.5 mm
C-14 dating: Kiel, CE 290 ± 25
Provenance: reportedly from Samangan Province, northern Afghanistan
Published: Carter / Goldstein 2013, cat. 98

Inv. no. LNS 74 R

The similarity between the creature represented on the previous example and this fantastic creature is so great that one might at first glance be tempted to interpret them as fragments of the same carpet. Here, too, one encounters a blue head with wide-open curling snout revealing traces of teeth, and ears jutting forward, although in this example the creature has a yellow tongue, a red-and-yellow striped ruff and a more pronounced mane. The dark brown outline of the body is almost too obtrusive, giving added emphasis to the lion-like tail.

A border fragment that was formerly erroneously attached to the long upper border of the carpet has proved to be part of the right-hand corner of the end-weave and has thus enabled the original width to be established. The white-ground field is relatively narrow and the long borders are very wide by comparison with the field. As on Cat. 1.7, the long borders feature a pattern of leafy scrolls on a blue ground, and a "wave-scroll" on the inner guard stripe. The red selvedge can be identified on the original end-weave of the upper edge.

The fundamental difference between these two animal carpets lies in their colourways, although it remains possible that they formed a pair. However, the alignment of the animals makes it clear that the two carpets were not intended to be laid out parallel to one another, as would have been the case if, for example, they had they been leading up to a throne.

I should like to conclude with a comment or two on the animal motifs. If the heads had been portrayed with greater precision, these mythical beasts might have been easier to identify; the generally crude nature of the weaving, however, precludes such accuracy. If we consider other highly regarded examples of Sasanian decorative arts, such as silverware, we find that figurative motifs are often clumsily rendered, with no attempt at naturalism, but at the same time there is always painstaking attention given to specific details.[16] Galloping horses, running deer, flying arrows, and details such as hooves, claws and open mouths are generally meticulously portrayed.

Cat. 1.9 AN ANIMAL COMBAT SCENE
**Eastern Iran,
5th–6th century CE**

Reconstructed
 length: *c.* 180 cm (warp direction),
 width 130 cm
Fragment a: length 105 cm, width 98 cm
Fragment b: length 58 cm, width 38 cm
Fragment c: length 31 cm, width 24 cm
Fragment d: length 51 cm, width 35 cm
Fragment e: length 22 cm, width 23 cm
 Warp: wool, white and brown, Z2S
 Weft: wool, 3Z
 Knots: wool, Z, 2–6 threads, V 11, H 14
 Back: one row of thick woollen yarn or
 strips of felt (light-coloured,
 white), attached every three
 rows of knots
 Selvedge: wool, light-coloured and brown.
 Long yellow fringes of wool on
 all sides, Z2S, attached to the
 long sides with brown yarn.
 So-called "false" fringes run
 along both edges in the direction
 of the weft. Kilim end turned
 under at least 7 cm and stitched
C-14 dating of
 fragment a: Zürich, CE 338 ± 28
Provenance: reportedly from Samangan
 Province, northern Afghanistan

 Inv. no. LNS 67 R a–h

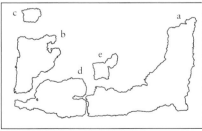

Fragment a

This fragment includes a complete section of the border, as well as a corner of the carpet. The red ground of the field is framed on its three remaining sides by a blue and an orange stripe interrupted by the snout of a strutting ram. Its snout, the edge of its abdomen and the inside of its raised foreleg are white, whereas the paw that encroaches on the lower stripes is blue. The main border with its dark blue ground is edged on the side of the field by a red-and-white "wave-scroll" guard stripe, and is decorated with lobed split-leaf scrolls, arranged in pairs on the narrow end, whereas on the long side they form a continuous reciprocal scroll. Halved blossoms with stubby white petals are placed at regular intervals along the inner edge of the border. The broad, yellowish-brown end-weave stripe is unusual in that it runs along both the horizontal and vertical edges, which creates the rather unusual effect of a fringe encircling the whole carpet.

Fragment d

Following on from the long lower edge of the previous fragment, this fragment includes the base line of the main motif, as well as the full width of the border and a small area of the field. Two lion's paws with distinct white claws encroach on the blue-and-yellow stripe and reach deep into the "wave-scroll" guard stripe. The halved blossoms placed at regular intervals along the outer edge of the border allow us to determine that the fragment featuring the lion's paws was originally positioned just a few centimetres away from the ram fragment. It is even conceivable that the lion was poised to attack the ram from the rear.

 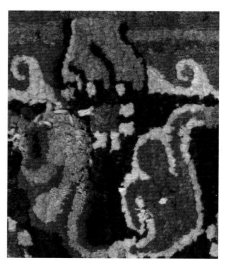

Detail of blossom, Cat. 1.9 (LNS 67 R), fragment b (left); detail of lion's paw encroaching in guard stripe, Cat. 1.9 (LNS 67 R), fragment d (right)

Scenes of animal combat stand in the broadest sense within the Persepolis tradition, which was present in the work of Persian craftsmen from antiquity, through to the Sasanian period and well into the Safavid period.

Fragment b
This vertical border originally must have been situated just behind the hind paw of the lion. It is not possible to reconstruct the exact distance from the base line, but it cannot have been very far removed because its lower edge includes a brown segmented band that may, I believe, have been the tip of the lion's tail. Directly above is a pair of tulips sprouting from a horizontal stem and oriented in opposite directions.

Fragment c
This small fragment marks the top left corner of the carpet, and features portions of the paired leaves from the border scroll against the blue ground.

Fragment e
The yellow and red stripes featured on this fragment resemble the end of a Sasanian filet or perhaps a flower; however, since there are no related motifs in the other fragments I shall have to forego any attempt to place this fragment.

Fragments f and g
These fragments regrettably amount to little more than tangles composed of knotted wool, warp yarns and pieces of backing material.

Cat. 1.9 (LNS 67 R), fragment f (left); fragment g (right)

Cat. 1.10 CORNER FRAGMENT
Eastern Iran, 4th–6th century CE

Length: 41 cm, width 55 cm
Warp: wool, white, occasionally brown, z2s, wavy
Weft: wool, z, 3 and 2x straight
Knots: wool, z, 2–3 s, asymmetrical, v 18, H 14
Back: wool, light-coloured, z, yarn attached in rows, very thick – up to 5 mm across and 4.5 cm long
Ends: Below, white kilim end, 7 cm minimum, folded under and sewn. Rounded left upper corner, over a thick warp bundle in alternating white and brown. Untrimmed yellow fringes applied on all sides, covering the selvedge in alternating white and brown
C-14 dating: Oxford, CE 329 ± 27
Provenance: reportedly from Maimana, Faryab Province, northern Afghanistan

Inv. no. LNS 63 R

Although it is quite clear that this example comprises a corner of a border and a small portion of the field, this thick and very heavy fragment poses some problems of interpretation regarding its pattern and function.

The main red band features the familiar pattern of paired scrolling trefoils, and chequered pyramidal forms related to the motifs featured on Cat. 1.13 and Cat. 1.5 fill the intervening areas. The guard stripe once again consists of a "wave-scroll" motif in white punctuated with blue against a red ground, and the dark brown field is framed with an ochre and red band.

Amid the confusion one can make out light blue, orange and white surfaces outlined in red, although their relationship to one another is unclear. The remaining areas are just as obscure, and the apparently charred area halfway up is breaking off.

Detail of paired scrolling trefoils

Cat. 1.11 A FELINE'S HEAD
Eastern Iran, 6th century CE

Length: 18 cm, width 22 cm
Warp: wool, white, z2s, wavy
Weft: wool, 1st weft z2, 2nd weft z1
Knots: wool, z3–5, asymmetrical, v 25, h 16
Back: wool, white and brown (goat's hair?)
One row of loops after every three
rows of knots
C-14 dating: Kiel, CE 437 ± 23

Inv. no. LNS 70 R

This lively feline head, which one might assume represents a tiger or a leopard on account of the blue streaks on its pelt, appears to be stalking a prey and about to inflict the first bite. Its laid-back ears, wide-open eyes and open jaw revealing white-and-orange teeth serve to emphasize the animal's fierce demeanour.

The inner guard stripe of the border features an orange "wave-scroll" punctuated with white against a blue ground, but the preserved portion of the main border is regrettably insufficient to allow the pattern to be identified.

The attacking feline motif is typical of a hunting carpet, which would usually feature several lions, or prey animals such as deer or antelope.

**Cat. 1.12 FRAGMENT WITH
A STAG HEAD**
Eastern Iran, 6th century CE

Fragment a: length 51.5 cm, width 49 cm
Fragment b: length 13 cm, width 13 cm (red)
Fragment c: length 13 cm, width 11 cm
(green and red)
Warp: wool, white, Z2S
Weft: wool, 2Z, 2x
Knots: wool, 4Z, asymmetrical, V 15, H 18
Back: wool, light-coloured and thick,
z and "unspun" yarn inserted after
every three rows of knots. Worn
down to the weave in many areas
Selvedge: one warp tightly overcast, with
brown fringes formed from the
outermost row of knots, which
have not been cut
C-14 dating: Kiel, CE 527 ± 27

Inv. no. LNS 71 R

This animated stag holding a pomegranate or blossom in its snout carries the weight
of its large antlers with great elegance. Adjacent to the stag a bluish-green surface
that appears to be the hindquarters of a creature with an upturned tail remains
difficult to identify, particularly since the shape does not seem to resemble any other
existing examples. Any attempt at interpreting it thus remains highly speculative.

In reconstructing the border, however, we are somewhat more fortunate.
Its blue ground is filled with a stretched scroll of lobed leaves in different colours.
A white "wave-scroll" punctuated with blue on a red ground serves as the inner
guard stripe, while the outer guard stripe consists of a horizontal band of coloured
chevrons. Two tiny, almost square fragments ("b" and "c") probably belong close
to the larger fragment, but do not cast any light on its motifs.

The colours of this carpet must once have been very vivid, because even in their
present condition they are still striking.

Cat. 1.13 STAGS FROM A ROYAL HUNT
Eastern Iran, 5th–6th century CE

Fragment a: length 180 cm, width 97.5 cm
Fragment b: length 28.5 cm, width 24.3 cm
      Warp: wool, white and brown, z2s, wavy
      Weft: wool, white, z3
     Knots: wool, 3z, asymmetrical, V 15, H 11
      Back: felted unspun wool, light and dark,
          attached after every three rows of
          knots
      Ends: 2 cm of kilim folded under and sewn.
          The first row of knots remains uncut
  Selvedge: warp overcast with wool in light-
          coloured and brown sections,
          with long, overhanging knots on
          both long sides
C-14 dating: Toronto, CE 420 ± 50
Provenance: reportedly from Maimana, Faryab
          Province, northern Afghanistan
Published: Carter / Goldstein 2013, Cat. 99

Inv. no. LNS 62 R a–b

Fortunately the field of this carpet is sufficiently well
preserved to be described easily. Leading the herd is a deer
sporting the Sasanian royal filet, which, according to the
prominent Russian scholar Boris Marshak, indicates that
the scene represents a royal hunt, but I am of the opinion that
the animals' postures pose a few problems of interpretation.[17]
On one hand, I am inclined to think that since the stags'
legs are curled under them it might suggest that they are in
a resting posture; on the other hand, given that their heads
are held up high, it would appear as though they are on the
alert.[18] Moreover, even though the horizontal filet and the
outstretched necks seem to imply that the animals are running
at speed, had this been the case, I believe the hind legs would
have been extended straight behind the body.

The four animals that have been preserved all have reddish-brown pelts and the extant massive and ornate antlers, as well as the hooves, are rendered in off-white. The nose of the first stag encroaches on the inner guard stripe, a stylistic device that is seen quite frequently, as for example in Cat. 1.9 where the snout of the ram interrupts the border.

The simple border design is familiar from other carpets. The main band has a pattern of black-and-white stepped crenellations, and is edged on the outside by a red-and-white chequered band, and on the inside by a "wave-scroll" motif.

Based on the rather limited material accessible to us at present, it would be risky to identify any determining features. A few clues, however, are available: the stag motifs are relatively crude; the colouration is unvaried; and the plain red ground does not feature additional small motifs, let alone any indication of vegetation. It would thus be premature to infer that the carpet is "early" or "late", but if we were to remain within the given Sasanian period, it would seem safest for now to accept the scientific dating to the fifth to sixth century CE.

This may be a suitable moment for another stylistic observation. In our first example of a carpet with stag motifs (Cat. 1.1), animals of the same type are represented within a network of compartments; a type of design that can be traced back to the Pazyryk carpet. In the present example, however, the animals are much more lively and unconfined, and portrayed in a style reminiscent of a hunting scene from the Taq-i Bustan rock reliefs, on the wall of the large *iwan* in which prey animals are depicted in naturalistic poses, and which was created between the fourth and fifth centuries CE.[19]

Detail of border, Cat. 1.9 (LNS 62 R)

Detail of stags, Cat. 1.9 (LNS 62 R)

Cat. 1.14 COMPARTMENT CARPET WITH FELINES
Iran, 6th–7th century CE

Fragment a: length 108 cm, width 70 cm
Fragment b: length 39 cm, width 40 cm
Fragment c: length 23 cm, width 52 cm
Fragment d: length 25 cm, width 16 cm
Fragment e: length 27 cm, width 16 cm
Warp: wool, white and brown z2–4s, wavy
Weft: wool, white and brown, z2–4s, straight
Knots: wool, 3z, asymmetrical, V 16, H 10 Pile height 1–1.5 cm
Back: no knotting
Ends: kilim edge on fragment c: wool, white, turned back at least 2 cm and sewn
C-14 dating of fragment a: Oxford, CE 470 ± 35; Zürich, 505 ± 50
Provenance: reportedly from Samangan Province, northern Afghanistan

Inv. no. LNS 48 R a–e

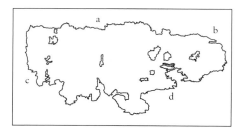

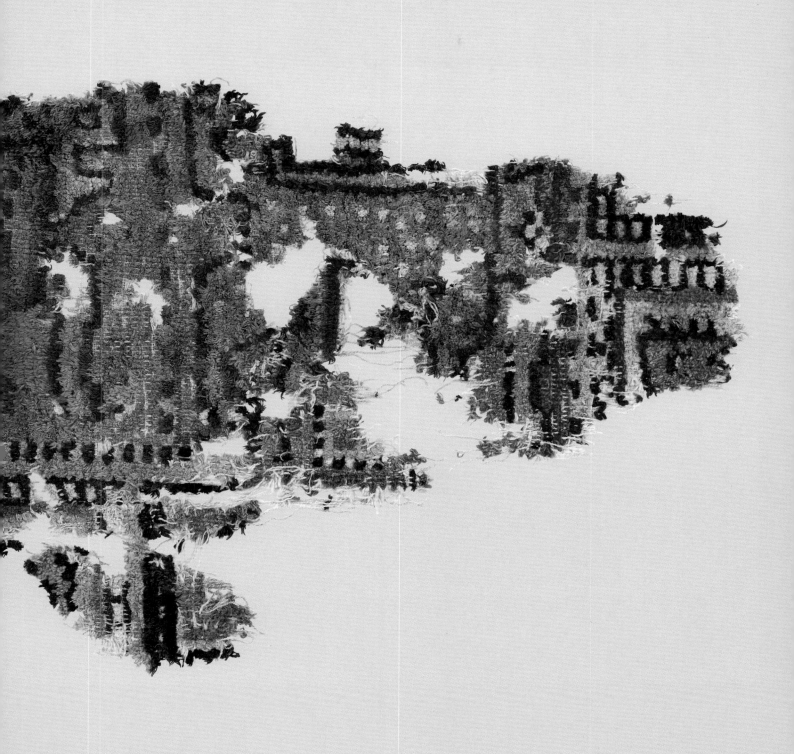

As mentioned earlier, compartmentalized fields of this type hark back to a pre-Sasanian tradition (see Cat. 1.1). The entire ground of the carpet is red, and the rectangular, almost square compartments of the field are bordered with dark-brown-and-white striped bands. A tiger whose pelt was originally probably rendered in off-white with dark brown streaks and is now almost light brown, stands in the left-hand compartment. Although its mouth is wide-open and its tail is upright, it does not appear poised to attack. The adjoining compartment contains a partially preserved feline of identical outline, but the spots on its olive-green pelt suggest that it is a leopard. The pose of both animals might be described as statue-like, and reflects little of the feline's natural elegance. Facing the felines are small motifs, which represent vegetation.

Surrounding the two main compartments along the lower border, and on the left-hand side of the fragment, are smaller rectangular compartments framed by blue-and-white striped bands. Comparable rectangles forming borders are familiar to us through several other examples, such as Cat. 1.1, although by comparison with the field compartments, those around the border are unusually large.

According to the placement of the fragments, the width of the original carpet, in the direction of the warp, must have been around 180 cm. The reconstruction of the length, in the direction of the weft, is based on the blue-and-white bands that outline the smaller compartments, which can be seen on the outer left side of the adjoining fragment "c" before the red end-stripe, and which recur in the top left corner of fragment "a". A greater length could only be conceivable if one excluded the border frames, creating space for one or two additional rows of compartments.

The lack of knotting on the back and the rather crude weave make this carpet seem thin and loose in comparison with the other examples shown here.

Detail of tiger, Cat. 1.14 (LNS 48 R), fragment a

Cat. 1.15 A MYTHICAL CREATURE AND THREE BORDER FRAGMENTS
Eastern Iran, 6th–7th century CE

Fragment c: length 34 cm, width 34.5 cm
Fragment d: length 42.5 cm, width 27 cm (snake's tail)
Fragment e: length 17.5 cm, width 12 cm ("running-dog"), continuation of fragment d
Fragment f: length 82 cm, width 61 cm (griffin)
Warp: wool, white, 2z, wavy
Weft: wool, z2–6 for one weft sequence
Knots: wool, 5–6z and also 2z, asymmetrical, V 15, H 14
Pile: in places up to 7 mm high, but also partly worn away
Provenance: reportedly from Samangan Province, northern Afghanistan

Inv. no. LNS 61 R c–f

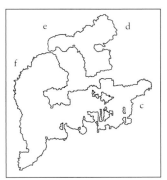

It is very likely, although not certain, that these four fragments belong together. Fragment "f", the most imposing of the group, is notable for its striking animal motif, and evidently belongs in the lower right-hand corner of the carpet.

The abdomen, hind leg and part of the foreleg of the spotted bluish creature are rendered in a lively fashion and outlined in white and red. The yellow striped wing is detailed with a chequered panel on the shoulder, and the curving neck appears to be bordered by a mane, both details associating it with the mythical creatures featured in Cat. 1.7 and 1.8.

A red "wave-scroll" guard stripe edges on the main border that features the familiar split-leaf scrolls expansively set against a blue ground and curling boldly in both directions. The thin knots on the far edge could be seen as a continuation of the "wave-scroll" or – my preferred theory – as the beginning of the vertical border. A blue band with a double row of white dots leads to another red area with a blue rectangular or octagonal form, which is difficult to interpret. A second, additional border or an unusually wide guard stripe would both be unprecedented in my experience, but we do not have enough comparable material to discount such a variation entirely.

Fragment "d" includes parts of a "wave-scroll" motif, alongside which appears to be a curved and slightly tapering tail with yellow scales or spots. It may perhaps have belonged to a dragon-like creature, but we cannot be sure.

Fragment "c" includes the same "wave-scroll" motif, as well as small squares enclosing chequered rosettes on a blue ground.

Fragment "e" is very small, and may well be the continuation of the "wave-scroll" motif mentioned above.

Detail of winged creature, Cat. 1.15 (LNS 61 R), fragment f

Cat. 1.16 **TWO BORDER FRAGMENTS**
Eastern Iran, 6th–7th century CE

Fragment a: length 24 cm, width 28 cm,
            possibly part of Cat. 1.14
Fragment b: length 17.5 cm, width 15.5 cm
    Warp: wool, Z2S, white and brownish
    Weft: wool, Z4–5
    Knots: wool, Z4, V 24, H 9
    Back: Z2S, one row of woollen yarns
          3–4 cm long, attached every three
          rows of knots
Provenance: reportedly from Samangan Province,
            northern Afghanistan
C-14 dating of
fragment "a": Oxford, CE 486 ± 27

    Inv. no. LNS 61 R a–b

These two fragments differ from the four other fragments (c–f) that share the same inventory number. There are no technical or stylistic similarities between the two groups, other than that they apparently came together from the same source and were thus inventoried at the same time.

Fragment "a" cannot be categorized, except that it retains part of a "wave-scroll" motif, whereas we can at least speculate that fragment "b" retains traces of a cable-motif border and bands of parallel lines, and may belong to the same group as Cat. 1.14. If so, the knots on the back would have been very irregular.

SASANIAN FLATWEAVES

The pile carpets described above, whose robust structure suggests that they were used by nomads as a protection against the cold ground, are the main focus of the remarkable al-Sabah holdings of Sasanian carpets.

In a nomadic context, flatweaves probably served as all-purpose textiles. For a long time virtually nothing was known about their use in the Sasanian period, which was probably due to their rarity and their simple designs, which did not attract much attention from collectors.

Based on Trudy Kawami's presentation[20] of the predominantly Sasanian textiles found in 1967 in Shahr-i Qumis, Khorasan, two fragmentary examples were reproduced in *Hali* in 1991: a double-woven brown and white example with vertical bands and a *zile* flatweave in wool and cotton with horizontal stripes, whose Persian origin is dubious and which may well have been imported, particularly since it included cotton.[21] There are similar question marks over the "pile carpet" fragment found during the same excavation:

based on my studies of the al-Sabah pile carpets (although I have not had the opportunity to study the original) I find it difficult to view the confused, monochrome, unpatterned, so-called "pile side" as anything but a standard padded backing, although this would mean that the face is an unpatterned flatweave.

Sasanian silverwork depicts flatweaves more frequently than carpets, with the flatweaves generally either displayed as saddlecloths, especially when of semicircular or rectangular shape,[22] or as cushions for couches or daybeds.[23] The most frequently used decorative motif centres on rosettes in patterns that variously fill the field of the flatweaves. The rosettes may be four-lobed, six-lobed, have heart-shaped petals or be spotted. Simple, geometric, linear patterns composed of diagonal or horizontal and vertical lines are also featured, as are "tiger stripes" and the motif of three dots arranged into a triangle. Saddlecloths are generally finished with a narrow border, whereas cushions are usually represented with no borders.

Cat. 1.17 WEFT-PATTERNED
FLATWEAVE CUSHION
Eastern Iran, 6th–7th century CE

Length: 56 cm, width 67 cm
(total length 112 cm, width 67 cm)
Warp: wool, white, Z2S
Weft: wool, many-coloured weft pattern,
3–4Z
Thread count: forty warps per 5 cm,
thirty-nine wefts per 5 cm
Weft pattern across 2–4 warps
Sides: turned back and sewn
C-14 dating: Toronto, CE 520 ± 60
Provenance: reportedly from Samangan Province,
northern Afghanistan

Inv. no. LNS 1085 T

Although both faces of this cushion are divided into square-shaped panels by fine vertical bands, the actual decoration was laid out to be viewed as horizontal bands of uninterrupted patterns.

Bands of ochre, red, olive-green and blue zigzags alternate with three bands of varying lozenge-shaped motifs set on point, two of which are rendered in the same colour variation as the zigzag band, and the third in red, blue and olive-green. The weaving technique has meant that all the patterns have a white ground.

As mentioned above, this relatively simple design corresponds with those seen on the daybed cushions illustrated on Sasanian silverware.[24] Moreover, as we have not been able to find a single example depicting an animal motif within a pearl roundel from the same source, we may therefore conclude that roundel motifs were only used on silk textiles that were made into garments, whereas Sasanian cushions were usually fashioned from woollen flatweaves.

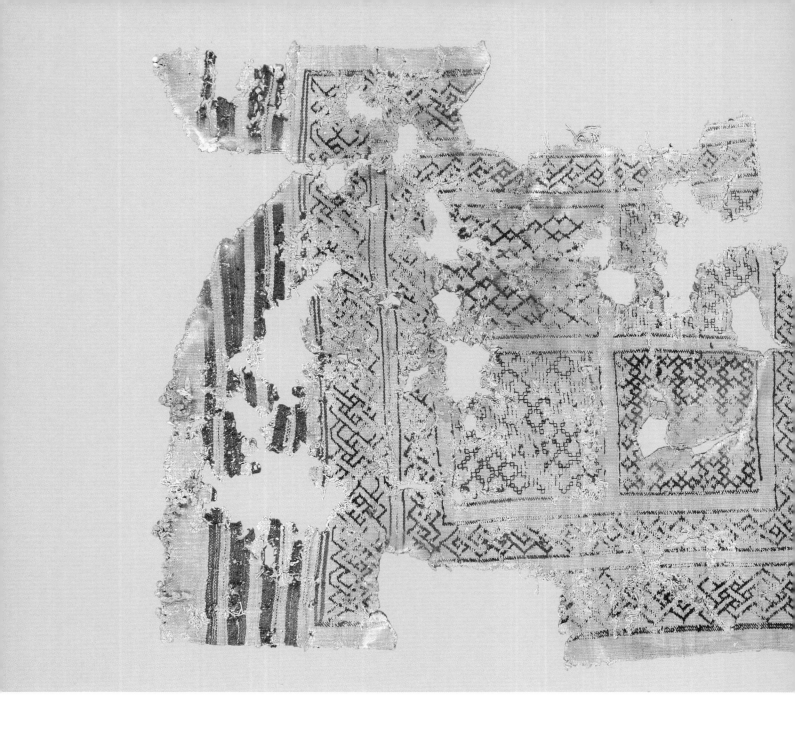

Cat. 1.18 FLATWEAVE RUG
Eastern Iran, 7th–8th century CE

Length: 300 cm, width 144 cm
Warp: wool, white and brown mix, S2Z
Weft: wool, predominantly brown, S1, weft pattern mostly across four warps
Sides: weft shoots wrapped over a warp bundle and turned over
Ends: broad white kilim ends with warp tassels knotted many times
C-14 dating: Kiel, CE 993 ± 25
Provenance: reportedly from Balkh, northern Afghanistan

Inv. no. LNS 72 R

This carpet's field is divided into two large square-shaped panels, each of which is sub-divided into four smaller panels, and one smaller rectangular panel equivalent to one half of the larger panels. The field is bordered by a wide band of plaited lozenges, and narrower bands of angular interlace run in-between the square-shaped and rectangular panels. Edging the narrow ends of the rug are striped bands of varying width.

The patterns enclosed in the small panels all centre around networks of lozenges and clearly aim to re-create a trellis, but do not seem to follow a regular repeat pattern. Four different filler patterns can be distinguished, arranged as follows:

1	2	3	4	2
2	4	2	1	4

Pattern 1 can be found in two fields and consists of a lattice of large overlapping lozenges, forming small lozenges on two points of intersection; pattern 2 is repeated in four fields and is comprised of a lozenge network made up of lines of minute lozenges; pattern 3 is depicted only once, and consists of loosely interwoven diagonal bands; pattern 4 is related to pattern 1, in that it is based on overlapping lozenges, but in this case the lozenges form smaller lozenges on four points of intersection.

The technique marks this carpet as a flatweave. The motifs are executed in monochrome brown wool running parallel to the weft against a woven ground of white wool. Usually the yarn is passed over three or four warps, then turned under a warp before the 3–4 rhythm is resumed.

The relatively simple pattern of the weave employs the decorative language of floor mosaics and thus provides an ideal design for a ground cover. Its undistinguished and therefore timeless patterns provide no useful evidence for dating, so we find ourselves compelled to follow the Carbon-14 analyses of this and the following almost identical example, which suggest dates between the sixth and the tenth centuries CE.

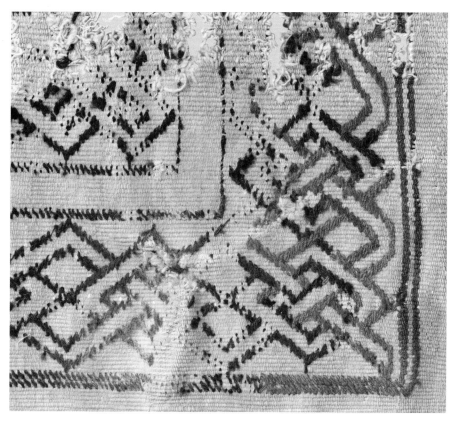

Detail of plaited border, Cat. 1.18
(LNS 72 R)

Opposite: Detail of patterns 3 and 4,
Cat. 1.18 (LNS 72 R)

Cat. 1.19 FLATWEAVE RUG
Eastern Iran, 7th–8th century CE

Length: 275 cm, width: 133 cm
Warp: wool, white and black-brown, z2s
Weft: wool, black-brown and pale, z
C-14 dating: Oxfordshire, CE 580 ± 40
Provenance: reportedly from Samangan Province,
northern Afghanistan

Inv. no. LNS 78 R

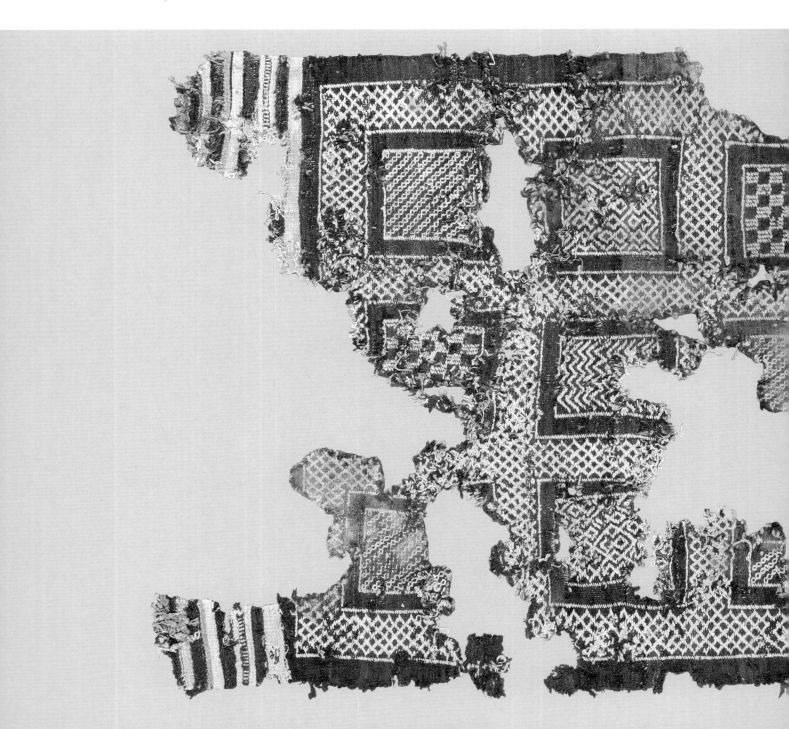

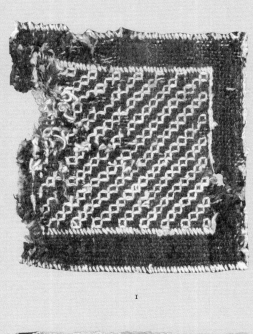

1

2

3

4

5

6

Unlike the closely related flatweave that precedes it, the field division of this example is much simpler and lacks the distinctive border bands. Here the field is divided into three rows of five square-shaped panels on a reserved diagonal grid. Six different patterns, clearly aiming at re-creating a trellis, decorate the squares but once again do not follow an identifiable rhythm:

1	2	3	4	5
3	6	1	2	6
1	2	1	4	5

Pattern 1 is comprised of diagonal bands of small abutted lozenges; pattern 2 repeats the pattern of overlapping lozenges related to the motif of the previous example, but here the large lozenges enclose two small interlaced lozenges; pattern 3 features a brown and white chequered motif; pattern 4, a honeycomb pattern; pattern 5, a network of lozenges enclosing smaller dotted lozenges; and pattern 6, a zigzag pattern.

The field is edged on the narrow sides by a broadly striped kilim end with plain and striped bands, and plain brown bands run along the long sides of the field to the kilim ends.

As with the preceding flatweave, we can only reach a date through the use of Carbon-14 analysis. In general terms, the simple patterns recall those seen on cushions depicted on Sasanian silverware.[25]

Details of patterns 1–6, Cat. 1.19 (LNS 78 R)

Cat. 1.20 DOUBLE-WEAVE FRAGMENT
Eastern Iran, 6th–7th century CE

Length: 19.5 cm, width 31 cm
Warp: wool, white and brown, Z2S
Weft: wool, various colours, Z,
1 shoot partly Z2, untwisted
Thread count: nineteen warps per 5 cm,
twenty-eight wefts per 5 cm,
great variations in thickness
C-14 dating: Oxford, CE 980 ± 27
Provenance: reportedly from Samangan Province,
northern Afghanistan
Literature: see Lamm 1937, pls. II and III

Inv. no. LNS 56 R

This small double-weave fragment is very simply patterned, and shows parts of parallel bands divided into rectangular compartments enclosing stylized angular rosettes. The red stripe is flanked on one side by a black stripe, and on the other with remains of a blue stripe. The black field seems to feature non-representational shapes in white, which could also be interpreted as floral motifs.

A fragment in the Sasanian decorative tradition in the Metropolitan Museum of Art displays some similarities with this example.[26] Although Maurice Dimand, the prominent curator of Near Eastern Art did not have access to Carbon-14 dating methods, which on this example point to the tenth century CE, he used stylistic comparisons to arrive at the relatively close date of the eighth to ninth centuries CE.

FRAGMENTS IN THE SASANIAN TRADITION

The rationale behind the grouping of these fragmentary pile carpets and flatweaves from the post-Sasanian period is twofold. Firstly, their shared place of discovery – Samangan in northern Afghanistan – suggests a connection with Sasanian examples; and secondly, the continuity of use for such textiles has also been demonstrated until well into the Islamic era.

In addition, these examples are so fragmentary that any classification as precursors to classical carpets cannot be supported. The two pile carpet fragments can be dated to the eleventh to twelfth and the twelfth to thirteenth centuries CE respectively, and the four kilims and the felt to between the ninth and thirteenth centuries CE.

Cat. 1.21 TWO BORDER FRAGMENTS
Eastern Iran (?),
11th–12th century CE

Fragment a: length 39 cm, width 24 cm
Fragment b: length 12 cm, width 14 cm
    Warp: wool, white, S2Z
    Weft: wool, wine red, 1st and 3rd shoots
        Z1, straight, 2nd shoot Z3, wavy
    Knots: wool, 2Z, symmetrical, V 51, H 29;
        some offset knots
C-14 dating: Oxford, CE 980 ± 27
Provenance: reportedly from Samangan Province,
        northern Afghanistan

Inv. no. LNS 58 R a–b

Without Carbon-14 dating techniques, it would be impossible to establish the age of these fragments. The rows of rounded corner rectangles enclosing concentric striped bands, which could be stylized representations of petals, have so little formal individuality that they could have been produced in any period – even as recently as the nineteenth century CE. An angular starburst rosette is featured in one corner of fragment "a", but even this provides no help in making an assessment.

The use of offset knotting suggests the Khorasan region, where this technique was in common use, at least in later centuries.[27]

Cat. 1.22 FRAGMENT WITH BIRD
**Eastern Iran,
12th–13th century CE**

Length: 25.5 cm, width 10.5 cm
Warp: wool, white, Z2S
Weft: wool, reddish, Z2
Knots: wool, Z2–4, symmetrical, V 28, H 25, some offset knotting
C-14 dating: Oxford, CE 1089 ± 26
Provenance: reportedly from Samangan Province, northern Afghanistan

Inv. no. LNS 54 R

Combining red, green, pale blue and apricot orange, the fragmentary motif on this example is practically impossible to decipher. With some imagination one could envisage it representing the neck of a bird (possibly a peacock), part of a bird's body and wing feathers. Stylized peacocks of this type recall examples of early Anatolian animal carpets, which followed the Seljuq style.[28]

Cat. 1.23 SLIT-WEAVE KILIM BORDER
Eastern Iran (?),
9th–10th century CE

Length: 30 cm, width 22 cm
Warp: wool, white, z2s
Weft: wool, z
Thread count: eleven warps per 5 cm,
eighty-two wefts per 5 cm
C-14 dating: Oxford, CE 762 ± 28
Provenance: reportedly from Samangan Province,
northern Afghanistan

Inv. no. LNS 55 R

The fragment displays warm abrash shades of dark blue ranging to a shade of bluish-green, coral, red and off-white, and was probably once part of a border. Red lozenges, outlined with off-white on a blue ground, are bordered on either side by broad red bands and fine blue bands. That which remains from the field is dominated by a lanceolate form, which with some imagination could perhaps be interpreted as an animal's eye.

The light-coloured section on the edge of the fragment might represent the lower end of the carpet.

We could not find anything comparable in other examples. At best there may be slight similarities with a few late Sasanian carpet fragments, particularly the stepped contours on Cat. 1.14; on the other hand, stepped contours are too common a feature to provide evidence of any connection.

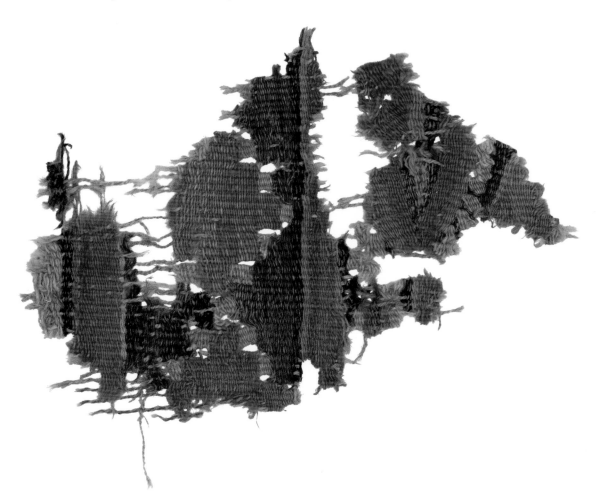

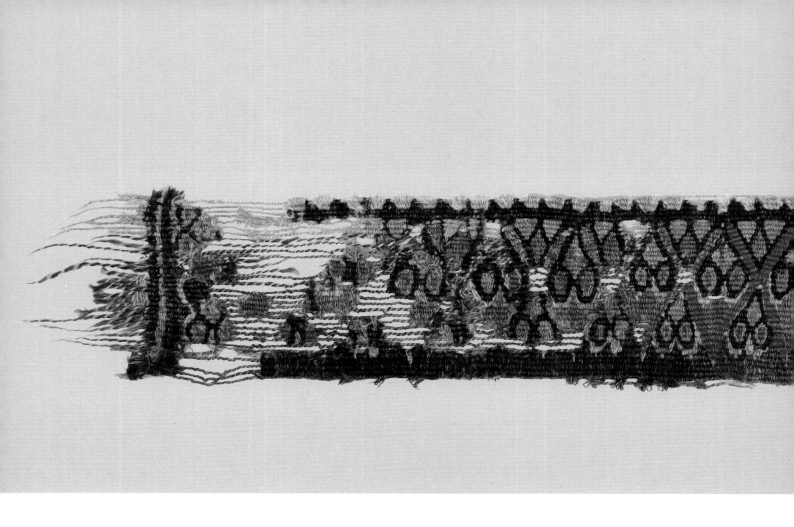

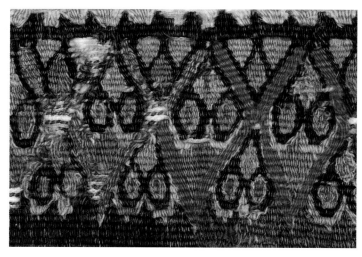

Detail of deltoid leaves, Cat. 1.24 (LNS 66 R)

Cat. 1.24 BORDER OF A SLIT-WEAVE KILIM
Eastern Iran (?),
9th–10th century CE

Length: 115 cm, width 16 cm
Warp: wool, light-coloured and light brown
Weft: weft pattern z and z2s
Thread count: thirteen warps per 5 cm,
eighty-nine wefts per 5 cm
C-14 dating: Oxford, CE 846 ± 27
Provenance: reportedly from Samangan Province,
northern Afghanistan

Inv. no. LNS 66 R

This long strip comprises a section of the left-hand border of a kilim with its original end-weave. The outermost edge is bordered with a plain blue band, and the inner stripe features a series of off-white dots showing some red from the field, especially on the upper right-hand edge of the fragment, where a small piece of the red flatweave field is still visible. The main border is decorated with staggered rows of blue deltoid leaves heightened with orange and red on a bluish-grey ground enclosed in red lozenges.

Such deltoid leaves or heart shapes are a familiar motif of the Sasanian decorative arts repertoire, and can likewise be found further west in the mosaic floors of Khirbat al-Mafjar, an Umayyad palace in the Jordan Valley.[29]

**Cat. 1.25 FRAGMENT OF A
SLIT-WEAVE KILIM
Egypt or Eastern Iran,
11th century CE**

Length: 18 cm, width 17 cm
Warp: wool, white, z2s
Weft: wool, z, densely packed, cotton,
white (outline)
Thread count: twenty-eight warps per 5 cm,
ninety-five wefts per 5 cm
C-14 dating: Kiel, CE 1026 ± 27
Provenance: reportedly from Samangan Province,
northern Afghanistan

Inv. no. LNS 69 R

This kilim fragment is too small to permit a complete idea of the design; only a few details can be observed, and these are fairly disconnected. The horizontal green panel, bordered by what appears to be a descendant of the "wave-scroll" motif, encloses a red panel that is bordered by an orange crenellation and features a row of puzzling motifs that resemble vases. The original width of the band is impossible to establish. Closer inspection suggests that the motifs on the surrounding red ground are small animals.

The fragment terminates on the bottom with an unpatterned blue band that likewise appears to be bordered by a "wave-scroll" motif. It is possible that this piece formed part of a bag or cushion.

Were it not for its Carbon-14 dating to the eleventh century CE, I would never have dared suggest that this piece was so old. Because of the traces of white cotton, the fragment could just as easily have been found in Fustat. The goods that were once transported along the Silk Road, especially during the Tang era, included textiles from almost all contemporary places of production.

Cat. 1.26 **KILIM FRAGMENT WITH
"KUFIC" BORDER**
Eastern Iran (?),
12th–13th century CE

Length: 31 cm, width 32 cm
Warp: wool, brown and white, z2s
Weft: wool, z2
C-14 dating: Oxford, CE 1106 ± 26
Provenance: reportedly from Samangan Province,
northern Afghanistan

Inv. no. LNS 59 R

In 1979 the author Yanni Petsopoulos became the first to devote attention to kilims made with the unusual double-interlock tapestry method, and to associate this technique exclusively with the Iranian world, especially its eastern regions. These kilims differ from slit-weave examples in that adjacent areas of colour are interlocked during weaving, which makes these textiles particularly durable. In the nineteenth and twentieth centuries, this technique was particularly favoured by Bakhtiari weavers.

My assumption is that this strip with its brown ground and "floriated Kufic" band was originally part of a border, and the "inscription" appears to represent the typical "la'a" repetition frequently found on objects from the repertoire of Islamic art. This main section of the border is edged on the outside by a plain red stripe, and on the inside by a yellow and red dice-pattern stripe. Once again, without Carbon-14 analysis, I would never have dared to give this fragment such an early date.

I should like to conclude the description of these two pile-carpets and four kilim fragments with a general observation. Fragments such as these are difficult to ascribe conclusively to a particular era, but due to the currently undisputed results of Carbon-14 analysis, they have significance as a potential cornerstone for the understanding of similar textiles.

**Cat. 1.27 FELT FRAGMENT WITH
RECIPROCAL MOTIF**
Central Asia, 13th century CE

Length: 29.5 cm, width 12.5 cm
Material: brown wool felt with red-and-blue
  embroidered outlines
C-14 dating: Oxford, CE 1131 ± 26
Provenance: reportedly from Samangan Province,
  northern Afghanistan

Inv. no. LNS 60 R

This fragment is decorated with a symmetrical arabesque centred on a blue stylized sepal and bud motif flanked by scrolling vines that probably once covered the entire surface of the object. Remains of the red, orange and green fills of the arabesque, outlined with blue-and-red embroidery, can still be seen.

The design and the slightly curved lower edge suggest that this was once a rounded saddlecloth or cushion, and may have originated in Mongolia or further east.

PART 2

SASANIAN AND SOGDIAN TEXTILES

The loose attribution of this group of silks to "post-Sasanian/Sogdian" is a sign of the difficulties posed by the classification of these textiles. In early publications on Sasanian art, such as those by Friedrich Sarre, Arthur Upham Pope and Kurt Erdmann, the small number of known examples were attributed to Iran during the Sasanian era.[1] The initial assumption that the centres of weaving were Iranian seemed plausible in the pioneering studies of Sasanian art because of the representations on rock reliefs of Taq-i Bustan (Figs 2.2–2.9) and Naksh-i Rustam, dating from the reign of Khosrau II (r. CE 591–628). These reliefs depict an abundance of garments in such detail that they almost constitute a sampler of Sasanian textiles. The clearest published photographs, taken at the relatively late date of 1969, originate from an archaeological expedition organized by Tokyo University under the direction of the Japanese art historian Shinji Fukai.[2]

Doubts began to set in, however, as to whether the surviving early textiles truly dated from around the middle of the seventh century, or the end of the Sasanian era. For stylistic reasons, which were difficult to prove, scholars increasingly tended to favour a post-Sasanian origin, and so this term came to apply to textiles whose attribution extends into the ninth century CE. Nevertheless, the Iranian decorative influences remain indisputable.

The raw material for these silks came exclusively from China. Woven textiles, and thus motifs, travelled first from Iran to Sogdiana, where in Afrasiab (on the site of the modern city of Samarkand) and Panjikent (in western Tajikistan), for example, production was in the hands not only of local weavers but also of migrants from Iran.[3] Here, too, there is evidence

of the popularity of Sasanian art in the form of wall paintings (Fig. 2.1, 2.11). In a fifth-century Sogdian dwelling in Panjikent, there are wall paintings that depict textiles with motifs similar to those represented in the Taq-i Bustan rock reliefs (Fig. 1.7). Those including animal motifs – with or without pearl roundels – were evidently among the most popular. Eventually, these motifs found their way to China, as did many examples of Sasanian decorative arts, including glass and silverware. Now preserved among the national treasures of Japan, at the Shōsō-in in Nara, a silk brocade example decorated with pearl roundels serves as evidence of how far east these textiles travelled. Sogdian weavers also settled in China, a fact that renders the task of identifying a textile's place of origin even more difficult.

The decoration of these silks is relatively uniform. They are woven with simple aligned or staggered repeat motifs. However, one also finds paired animals, either confronted or addorsed, and sometimes only depicting the head of the animal. The pearl roundel primarily served a structural purpose. It was typically divided by four squares positioned at cardinal points that split the roundel into four segments of equal size – rather like the face of a clock. Another variant was composed of many smaller pearls in single or double rows, and a final variation comprised a chain of alternating conical and deltoid leaf or heart-shaped motifs (see pp. 150–51). Aside from paired horsemen (Cat. 2.1), the motifs within these enclosed divisions were all animals, and among these, single depictions were dominant. The range extends from the mythical, phoenix-like *senmurv*, through birds such as ducks, peacocks, pheasants and guinea fowl, to stags (or ibexes), goats, elephants and boars. They surely possessed some significance beyond their decorative properties, such as, for example, denoting the rank of those who wore the motifs on their garments. We owe the most detailed account of these textiles to the renowned textile specialist, Karel Otavsky, although he did not tackle the particular issue of rank badges.[4]

The most important Sasanian source is found on the left-hand side façade of the largest cave at Taq-i Bustan in southern Iran, which features large-scale scenes of a royal boar hunt.

Fig. 2.1 *opposite*
Ambassadors bearing gifts, detail from *The Hall of Ambassadors*, Afrasiab Museum, Samarkand, Uzbekistan, 7th century CE Courtesy of the Museum of History, Afrasiab, Uzbekistan. Photography courtesy of Dr Fabrizio Lombardi, Milan.

Fig. 2.2 *overleaf*
Relief of royal boar-hunting on the left wall of the Taller Grotto, Taq-i Bustan, Iran. From Shinji Fukai, *Taq-i Bustan: The Tokyo University Iraq–Iran Archaeological Expedition*, 1969, PL. XXXII.

Figs 2.3, 2.4 *above*
Details showing garments worn by the king in the relief-carving of a royal boar-hunting scene on the left wall of the Taller Grotto, Taq-i Bustan, Iran.
From Fukai, *Taq-i Bustan*, PL. L, LXIII and LXIV.

The figure of Khosrau II appears twice: once standing in a boat drawing his bow (Fig. 2.3); in the other, armed with a bow and getting ready to draw it (Fig. 2.4). In both scenes, the king wears a long caftan decorated with *senmurvs*. In the boat scene depicted on the right of the relief, he is shown reaching for an arrow and preparing to draw his bow. His trousers likewise appear to be decorated with a *senmurv* on each leg. His companions include an attendant whose garment is decorated with large crane motifs (Fig. 2.5), presenting an arrow; an oarsman at the rear of the boat, in a garment with a diagonal lattice of guinea fowl motifs, along with a boar's head in a simple roundel on his thigh (Fig. 2.6); and a helmsman, whose garments are unfortunately no longer distinct. A bird can be discerned on his left upper arm, and there are some un-patterned small roundels on his jacket-like outer garment.

In the boat scene depicted on the left of the relief, Khosrau is drawing his bow. Beside him a musician with a harp-like stringed instrument wears a caftan with large rosettes (Fig. 2.7, overleaf). The upper garment of the attendant in charge of arrows includes a pair of large confronted herons (Fig. 2.8, overleaf); and the oarsman's garment is decorated with guinea fowl or ducks within a diagonal lattice, as previously described.

These identical representations were a typical Sasanian device for emphasizing a timespan or the "before and after" of a specific scene, and also served to illustrate the fixed ranking of the garments worn by royal attendants.

In a third boat, on the upper left-hand side of the wall, a row of "beaters" clap their hands, a hunting strategy serving to drive the boar in the desired direction. Their caftans, which are belted at the waist, are decorated with rows of pheasants, ducks

Figs 2.5, 2.6 *above*
Details showing the garment worn by one of the king's attendants (Fig. 2.5) and by the oarsman (Fig. 2.6) in the relief-carving on the left wall of the Taller Grotto, Taq-i Bustan, Iran. From Fukai, *Taq-i Bustan*, PL LXVI and LXVII.

and peacocks. In the fourth boat – situated lower down, between the two Khosrau boat scenes – are five seated female musicians, whose garments are depicted with relative clarity. Where the details can be distinguished, the motifs are all rosettes.

Away from the boats, to the far left of the relief, the elephant riders are worthy of attention. The rider depicted on the top wears a garment decorated with ducks, upon which even the drake's upwardly curved tail feathers are clearly visible (Fig. 2.9, overleaf). Below is another rider whose garments feature ducks and birds that may be doves. Below him is a rider wearing a garment with pheasants and ducks; indeed these and doves are the only motifs to be seen in all five groups of elephant riders, who are probably members of the court.

There is no discernible difference between beaters and attendants as far as the choice of bird motifs is concerned,

and only the musicians wear rosettes instead of birds. Evidently the *senmurv* was reserved for the king alone.

Stags and wild boar were common prey for hunters, and are represented on the Taq-i Bustan rock reliefs. Both animals can be seen in pearl roundel motifs on our textiles.

This brief description of the various garments has not yet resolved the question of whether specific groups of people always wore garments featuring the same motifs – possibly functioning as blazons or as indications of social status. A basis for this interpretation can be found in the early Ming period, when Chinese military officials and civil servants wore emblems known as "mandarin squares" or "rank badges" on their outer garments, reflecting a strict hierarchy.[5] Nine different birds denoted civilian ranks, while nine other different animals were used for the military. However, it is not known whether a similar system was used on Sasanian textiles, and the Taq-i Bustan carvings do not provide enough evidence either way.

The corpus of post-Sasanian and Sogdian textiles comes for the most part from chance discoveries made in European church treasuries.[6] In the late nineteenth century, however, archaeological work carried out by museums in London, Paris and Berlin at locations including Dunhuang and Turfan in western China brought more of these textiles to light. The fourth and final expedition by Sir Aurel Stein in 1931 brought an end to these excavations, which until then had been organized largely by Europeans, but some thirty years later the Chinese continued the work begun in the Taklamakan Desert by Stein, Albert von Le Coq and Paul Pelliot. First, from 1959 onwards, the Institute of Archaeology of the Chinese Academy of Social Sciences led digs that excavated large numbers of textiles from burial sites. Then, in 1984,

the Sinologist Helga Natschläger completed her dissertation on polychrome silks found in Astana in Kazakhstan.[7] Her precise dating of the individual burial sites was an important step forward in establishing the age of the textiles. These *ante quem* dates are still the most trustworthy framework for dating available today, alongside Carbon-14 testing. The majority of Natschläger's thirty-eight examples dated from the second half of the Sasanian era, with a small number originating after CE 642. Between 1980 and 1987, the Institute of Archaeology in Xinjiang carried out further excavations, and their new finds considerably enhanced our knowledge of these early textiles. A detailed and thorough account of all these discoveries can be found in two publications written by Zhao Feng.[8]

Outside of China, greater awareness of the latest finds and of materials that had long remained unknown was created by the 1998 exhibition and catalogue *When Silk Was Gold* by James C. Y. Watt and Anne E. Wardwell.[9]

Figs. 2.7, 2.8, 2.9
Details showing the king's musician (Fig. 2.7, above left), the attendant with arrows (Fig. 2.8, above right), and the elephant rider (Fig. 2.9, opposite) in the relief-carving on the left wall of the Taller Grotto, Taq-i Bustan, Iran. From Fukai, *Taq-i Bustan*, PL LI, LIII and XXXIX.

TEXTILES FROM THE AL-SABAH COLLECTION AND THEIR ICONOGRAPHY

Parallel to the Sasanian-period pile-carpet fragments and sharing the same provenance, a considerable number of silk fragments have found their way to Kuwait. The majority of these were acquired at the turn of this century, with further individual finds expanding the collection in 2010. It can consequently be said that this is one of the most comprehensive private collections of these textiles in the world, and also provides us with an opportunity to study and discuss their subject matter and iconography that is unlikely to be repeated.[10]

Some nineteen of these examples form a corpus that consists almost exclusively of animal motifs. The exception, featured in two variants (Cat. 2.1 and Cat. 2.2), is a motif of paired riders on winged horses who are turning to confront each other. The animal motifs are enclosed, as we have mentioned earlier, within varying designs of pearl roundels. Similar motifs can be seen on Sasanian stucco tiles,[11] on silver vessels from the same period,[12] on stone seals,[13] and, last but far from least, on the wall paintings of Panjikent, where some figures are depicted wearing garments with pearl roundel designs (see pp. 16–17, Fig. 1.7).

The iconographic range of animal motifs is surprisingly broad, and can be divided into three categories: mammals, birds and fantastical creatures, as follows:

A) Mammals:
   A procession of horses: Cat. 2.4
   A procession of rams: Cat. 2.5
   Boar heads: Cat. 2.6, 2.7
   Confronted elephants: Cat. 2.9
   Confronted stags: Cat. 2.10, Cat. 2.11, Cat. 2.12
   Deer: Cat. 2.13

B) Birds:
   Peacocks, shown frontally: Cat. 2.3
   Ducks, single or paired: Cat. 2.14, Cat. 2.15
   Pheasants, single or paired: Cat. 2.16, Cat. 2.17
   Confronted guinea fowl: Cat. 2.19
   Flying birds (Tang Dynasty, China): Cat. 2.20

C) Fantastical animals:
   Senmurvs: Cat. 2.8
   Winged horses, with riders: Cat. 2.1, Cat. 2.2

The extensive scope of the textiles in The al-Sabah Collection can be gauged from the fact that only two of the animal motifs known to us from other examples are not represented here: the lion[14] and the bear.[15]

It would exceed the bounds of this catalogue to discuss the iconography of each individual animal, although as we have already indicated, this could provide us with a basis for allocating each one to a specific group of wearers.

**Cat. 2.1 FRAGMENTS OF
A GARMENT OR
A SADDLE BLANKET**
**China or Central Asia,
6th century CE**

Silk samite
Fragment a: length 42.5 cm, width 52 cm
Fragment b: length 29 cm, width 31 cm
C-14 dating of
fragment a: Kiel, CE 555 ± 25 (one sigma range:
CE 639–663, 64.2%)

Inv. no. LNS 1144 T a, b

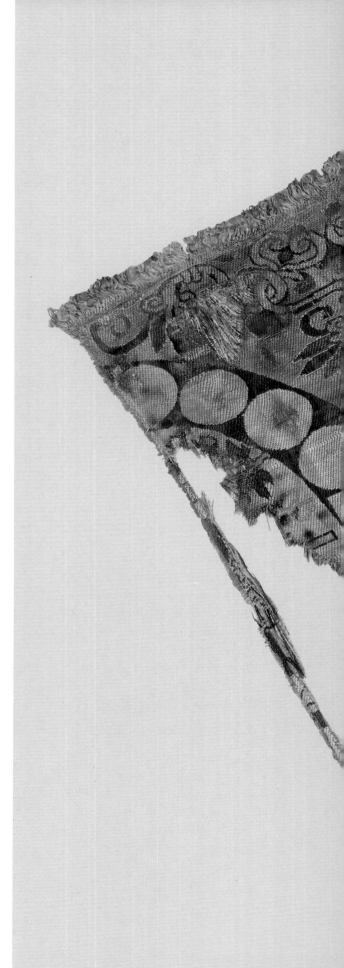

Both fragments are from the same textile, and, although no complete
pearl roundels have been preserved due to the numerous seams and
missing areas, the design is sufficiently clear to be reconstructed. The
cardinal points of each roundel are marked by rectangles allowing five
pearls in each quadrant. The roundel is divided into two symmetrical
halves by a tree with pomegranate fruit growing among its leaves. Each
half is almost completely filled by a winged horse galloping away from
the centre, with its rider facing the other rider and clinging to the neck
of the horse. The eyes of each rider are fixed intensely on the other,
suggesting an imminent duel. Their headdresses comprise caps with
turban-like beaded ornaments surmounted by a crescent on the front,
which, together with the riders' beards and moustaches, may indicate
that these are men of royal blood. Their wing-like shoulder ornaments
have no known counterparts in Sasanian art. Preserved on the left-hand
side of fragment "b", the horse's head with its slightly open mouth and
bent forelegs is extremely elegant. The horses are coloured in shades of
blue and bluish-green.

In the interstices of the roundels are elaborate foliate arabesques
apparently bearing circular green fruit. Although the centres of the
fragments are now missing, I presume that the horses would have had
knotted tails, as can be seen in Cat. 2.2, and do not wear filets of the
kind often represented in Sasanian art.

The banner of the Emperor Shomu (r. CE 724–748), which has
now been known for almost a century and is preserved at the Shōsō-in
in Nara, is undoubtedly an ancestor of these silk fragments.[16] Its design

Cat. 2.1 (LNS 1144 T), fragment a

demonstrates that the Byzantine-Sasanian style travelled as far afield as Japan, so we can be sure that it was also known and used as a motif in China prior to the middle of the eighth century CE. The banner features paired riders turning and drawing their arrows at lions that are attacking them from the rear. The simplified version used in Cat. 2.1 only depicts forceful riders turning in their saddles, but the reason for the expression on their faces is not shown.

The coarse and heavy texture of the textile suggests that it was not intended for a garment. It seems more likely that it was part of a curtain or wall hanging, or perhaps a saddle blanket.

Detail of interstitial foliate arabesques, Cat. 2.1 (LNS 1144 T), fragment a

Cat. 2.1 (LNS 1144 T), fragment b

**Cat. 2.2 SILK FRAGMENT
WITH PAIRED RIDERS
China or Central Asia,
5th–6th century CE**

Silk samite
Length: 30.5 cm, width 35 cm
C-14 dating: Kiel, CE 495 ± 25 (one sigma range:
CE 597–643, 65.6%; two sigma range:
CE 558–651, 94.4%)

Inv. no. LNS 1145 T

This variant of the paired horsemen motif matches the previous example, although minor differences in rendering, such as the foliate arabesque motif between the roundels, the riders' headdresses, and the colour variations in the bodies of the two winged horses, show that this fragment is not from the same silk. I could not find any other evidence for a different provenance or dating. The popularity of this motif is therefore apparent. As yet I cannot derive the specific use of this textile or the reason for its division into horizontal strips.

Cat. 2.3 **FRAGMENTS OF
A GARMENT**
**China or Central Asia,
6th–7th century CE**

Silk samite
Fragment a: length 26.5 cm, width 37 cm
Fragment b: length 31 cm, width 18.5 cm
Fragment c: length 24 cm, width 15 cm
C-14 dating: Kiel, CE 505 ± 25 (one sigma range:
CE 601–642, 68.3 %; two sigma
range: CE 571–650, 95.4 %)
Provenance: reportedly from Samangan Province,
northern Afghanistan

Inv. no. LNS 1174 T a, b, c

These beaded roundels are divided by four squares into four
equal sections comprising five pearls each. The enclosed motif is
symmetrical and dominated by a bird viewed frontally. Its bold
blue breast marks the centre of the roundel, and the two paler ovals
could, by analogy with other bird and animal motifs, be interpreted
as joints, but it is difficult to tell whether these belong to the
outstretched wings or the legs below. The wing-divisions or wing
bars are clearly marked by horizontal ornamental bands.

At the point where the plump breast tapers to the slender neck,
we see the quite common Sasanian-style pearl collar. The frontally
viewed head is difficult to discern, but there are indications that the
bird may be a peacock, as it appears to be wearing a small crown.
This also seems to be borne out by the luxuriant tail feathers with
their elaborate scrolls that could represent the "eyes" on peacock
plumes. Flanking the bird's head are two small snarling lions with
open jaws, about to pounce on two green parrot-like birds; these
lions appear to be related to the ones that are about to attack the
horse riders in the banner of the Emperor Shomu, which we have
previously discussed as an ancestor of Cat. 2.1 and Cat. 2.2
(see pp. 102–5).

The horizontal rows of roundels alternate with rows of
relatively large beaded medallions issuing four foliate motifs.

Cat. 2.3 (LNS 1174 T), fragment a

Cat. 2.3 (LNS 1174 T), fragment b

Cat. 2.3 (LNS 1174 T), fragment c

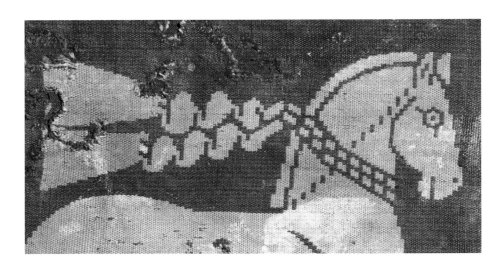

**Cat. 2.4 SILK FRAGMENT
WITH ROWS OF HORSES**
Eastern Iran, 5th–6th century CE

Silk samite
Length: 41 cm, width 48.5 cm
C-14 dating: Zürich, CE 435 ± 45
(sigma range N/A)
Provenance: reportedly from Samangan Province,
northern Afghanistan
Published: Carter / Goldstein 2013, cat. 100

Inv. no. LNS 548 T

Three rows of horses, facing in opposite directions, move in a horizontal procession across a cherry-red ground. There are no indications of a landscape. Running horizontally along the top of the silk fragment is a sharp fold marked by stitches from what was once a seam, indicating that this textile was probably part of a garment.

The elegant and well-fed horses all sport fluttering filets that are twisted around their necks and extend along the whole length of their bodies – a typical Sasanian motif signalling that these are not ordinary horses, and that the owner of the garment would have been a high-ranking personage. Additionally, smaller ribbons adorn the horses' knees and the middle of their tails.

Along with the naturalistic depiction of the white horses, the deep, glowing red of the ground is striking. This particular dye tends to react very strongly to the effects of time and burial under ground, and easily loses its colour. Very often all that remains is an insipid brown, as we shall see below (Cat 2.7).

The imposing appearance of a garment made from this textile is easy to envision.

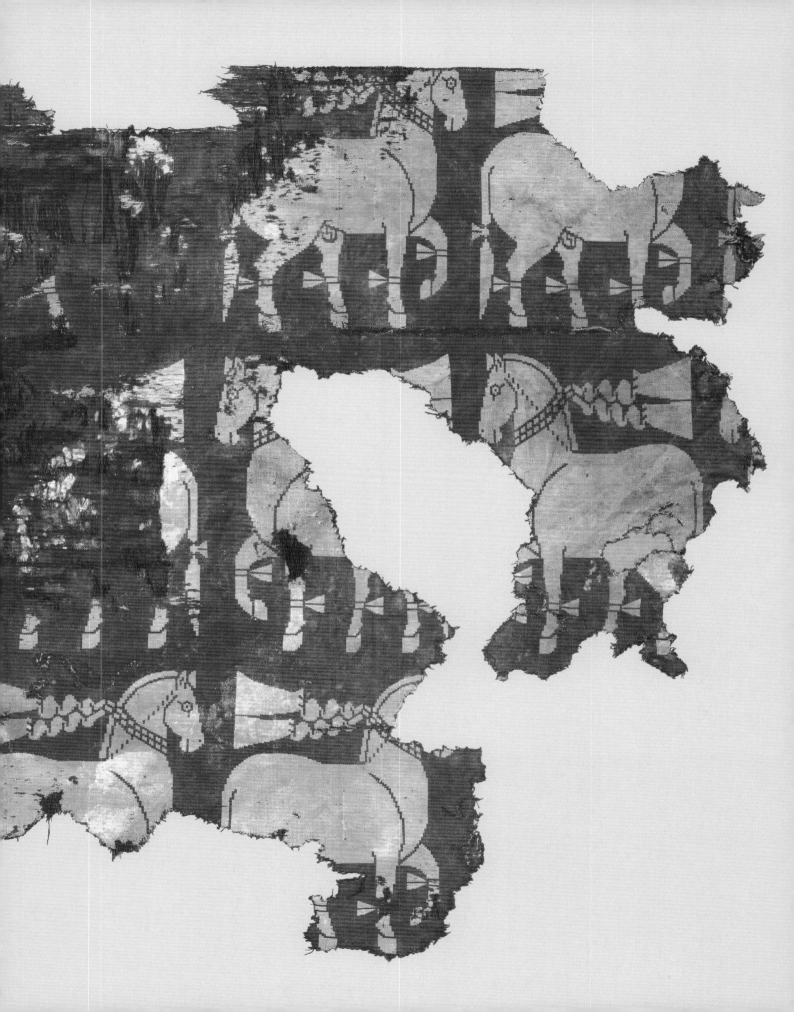

**Cat. 2.5 SILK FRAGMENTS WITH
A PROCESSION OF RAMS**
Eastern Iran, 5th–6th century CE

Silk samite
Fragment a: length: 23.5 cm, width 54 cm
Fragment b: length: 59 cm, width 12 cm
C-14 dating: Kiel, CE 385 ± 28 (one sigma range:
CE 462–522, 49.2%; two sigma range
CE 423–545, 91.6%)

Inv. no. LNS 1143 T a, b

Regal-looking rams facing to the left walk in a procession across the bottom of fragment "a". Their prominent horns curl symmetrically on either side of their heads, and their outsized collars – comprising a single row of pearls and a pendant – develop into a pair of filets that flutter over their backs. The narrow, wedge-shaped fragment "b" demonstrates that the rams change direction in each row.

A fragment bearing the same ram motif, found in Antinoë, Upper Egypt, ended up in Lyon during the nineteenth century.[17] In 1913, Otto von Falke attributed it to Iranian workshops, and this attribution was confirmed eighty years later by Leonie von Wilckens. In the meantime, a second, relatively large fragment (58 × 34 cm) with the same basic design as the Kuwait fragments appeared in the Katoen Natie collection in Antwerp.[18] As both of these fragments are large and show no indication of seams, it is not clear if they were used as garments, as was the case with the previous silk samites from the same period.[19] Furthermore, the blue border with its row of six-petalled rosettes may suggest that it was used as a curtain or wall hanging.

The lower selvedge is about a centimetre wide and is distinguished by a regular row of hanging threads, each about two centimetres long. Apparently another piece of fabric was once attached here; however, it bears no resemblance to the seam of a garment.

Fig. 2.10
Sasanian stucco tile with ram motif, Museum für
Islamische Kunst, Berlin, Inv. no. I.2212.
© bpk/Museum für Islamische Kunst.

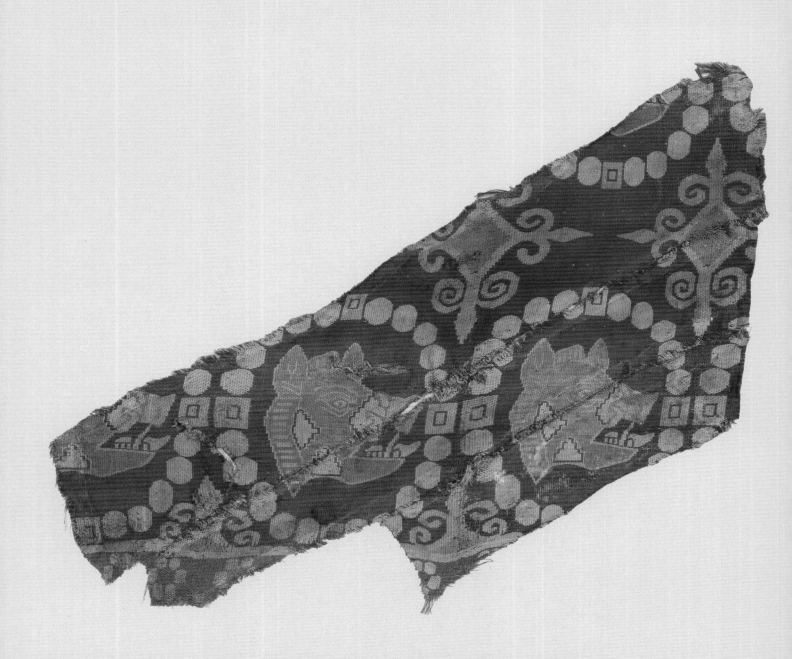

**Cat. 2.6 SILK FRAGMENT
WITH BOAR'S HEADS
Central Asia, 7th–8th century CE**

Silk samite
Length: 13.5 cm, width 33.5 cm
Three strips sewn together in the
direction of the weave: length 25 cm,
width 28 cm
Literature: Zhao Feng 1999, pp. 110–11

Inv. no. LNS 1136 T

In depictions of the popular royal pastime of hunting, the prey is often shown either fleeing or lying dead on the ground. The head of a wild boar with its menacing tusks was a highly prized trophy; it is therefore plausible that it could have been associated with royalty and is often used as a motif on princely garments (Fig. 2.11). Both rows of motifs on this fragment feature a repeating pattern of a pale blue boar's head, facing to the right, with pointed ears, looking ferocious with its mouth open and its tusks and tongue in full view. The surrounding pearl roundel is typically divided into five pearls per section, with four squares to mark the horizontal and vertical axes. The fleur-de-lis motif that appears between the roundels is also typical of Sasanian iconography. The row of halved fleur-de-lis motifs on the bottom of the fragment is bordered by a horizontal line that marks the beginning of the repeating roundel pattern, preceded by a border-like band composed of rows of small rosettes, each comprising six round lobes.

This fragment is made up of three strips of almost equal width, running at an oblique angle to the direction of the weave. It is difficult to picture how it could have formed part of a garment, though it is easy to imagine the intense red ground and the vivid boars' heads featuring on a royal robe.

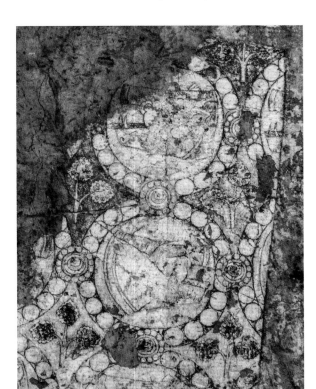

Fig. 2.11
Detail of a garment decorated with a similar boar's-head motif in the wall painting *The Hall of Ambassadors*, Afrasiab Museum, Samarkand, Uzbekistan, 7th century CE. Courtesy of the Museum of History, Afrasiab, Uzbekistan. Photography courtesy of Dr Fabrizio Lombardi, Milan.

Cat. 2.7 EMBROIDERED FRAGMENT WITH BOAR'S HEADS
Central Asia, 5th–6th century CE

Silk, embroidered
Length: 21.5 cm, width 40 cm
Chain-stitch on two layers of fabric: fine silk upper layer and coarse silk lower layer
C-14 dating: Kiel, CE 465 ± 25 (one sigma range: CE 558–605, 68.3%; two sigma range CE 542–635, 95.4%)
Provenance: reportedly from Samangan Province, northern Afghanistan
Literature: *Hali* 146, 2006, p. 64

Inv. no. LNS 1175 T

The top left corner of this fragment of chain-stitch embroidery, which is on two layers of fabric, may have been part of a blanket. A deltoid leaf enclosing a fleur-de-lis motif runs through the border, and we can see two boars' heads facing left inside pearl roundels. As in the previous example, and in other late Sasanian textiles with boar's head motifs, the animal's mouth is wide open, as if it is about to attack.

Between the roundels foliate volutes issue fleur-de-lis, a common interstitial motif on textiles with repeating roundels, and in the corner the same motif has been modified to accommodate the pearl roundel.

Burial underground has had a very damaging effect on the colours of this textile. A faded light blue or light green, as well as a pale yellow, can be distinguished against the dark red ground, which has now turned brown.

Cat. 2.8 GARMENT FRAGMENT
WITH *SENMURV* MOTIFS
Central Asia, 6th–7th century CE

Silk samite
Length: 27.2 cm, width 7.8 cm

Inv. no. LNS 1201 T

The *senmurv* motif can be seen adorning the garments of the two representations of Khosrau II in the Taq-i Bustan hunting scenes (Figs 2.3 and 2.4), and can also be found on a green caftan preserved in the State Hermitage Museum, St Petersburg,[20] and in a garment depicted in the wall painting from Afrasiab known as *The Hall of Ambassadors* (Fig. 2.12).

Although only one half of the roundel of this red-grounded fragment remains, it is clear that the other half would have been identical. The fierce-looking *senmurv* depicted in the roundel stands on a pedestal of split palmettes, a motif that can be found on many other textiles, and is always used as a base to support confronted animals. The depiction of this mythical creature is quite typical, but one unusual feature is the large number of small pearls that compose the roundel. The foliate interstitial motif is also typical of such textiles.

The long right-hand edge is clearly a selvedge, but the opposite edge shows traces of a seam, which makes it fairly certain that this was part of a garment. Interesting parallel examples can be found in the catalogue of the exhibition *La seta e la sua via*.[21]

Fig. 2.12
Detail of a garment decorated with a *senmurv* motif in the wall painting *The Hall of Ambassadors*, Afrasiab Museum, Samarkand, Uzbekistan, 7th century CE. Courtesy of the Museum of History, Afrasiab, Uzbekistan. Photography courtesy of Dr Fabrizio Lombardi, Milan.

Cat. 2.9 TEXTILE WITH ELEPHANTS
Central Asia, 7th century CE

Silk samite
Length: 157 cm, width 22.8 cm
Provenance: reportedly from China

Inv. no. LNS 1215 T

This strip, with its six vertical pearl roundels encircling confronted elephants, is in many respects a novelty within the group of Sasanian silk samites.

Among the textiles that found their way into church treasuries during the early Middle Ages, where they were primarily used to wrap precious relics, there are at least two examples of elephant motifs. Both were already known from the end of the nineteenth century, and since Falke's comprehensive account of silk-weaving – if not earlier – they have been classified as Byzantine-Sasanian.[22] During the past thirty years, no further Sasanian textiles with elephants have appeared on the art market, and yet they were once a familiar sight, as is evident from their frequent depiction in the Taq-i Bustan rock reliefs.

It was not until recently that this vertical strip and a horizontal one in the same style, featuring two-and-a-half pearl roundels, were discovered.[23] A pair of placid-looking Asian elephants stand confronted, on a pedestal of split palmettes, each with one foreleg raised, and with gently curving striped trunks that look somewhat reptilian. In this respect they match the above-mentioned examples that were brought to Europe many years earlier. The tusks are short and pointed, and the colour of the ears is variously red or yellow. Next to the elephants' small ears, at a slight angle, we can see their musth-gland secretions, a not uncommon feature in representations of elephants, and an indication that the weavers were familiar with this type of animal. The greatest source of variation is in the crown-like headdress above the dorsal bumps on the elephants' heads, and the beaded decorative bands below the dorsal bumps. This makes it clear that these elephants were not used for labour or for warfare, but for the entertainment of the royal court.

The requisite interstitial motifs, which are near-identical to the ones found on Cat. 2.8, consist of four cup-like red flowers, and although they are only half preserved because of the vertical cuts in the fabric, the precision and elegance of the workmanship is plain to see.

None of the sides of this strip include an original selvedge, but an edging strip, around 2 cm wide, borders all four sides of the fragment and consists largely of six individually sewn pieces of fabric in graduating colours. These, plus the evenness and lack of folds, make it clear that this textile could not have been part of a garment. Since a shorter, horizontally orientated example is also known, we could consider the possibility that it was part of a wall-hanging; however, it might just as easily have been part of a banner of the type (*thangka*) often found in Tibetan monasteries. There were no indications of this being an archaeological find.

Detail, Cat. 2.9 (LNS 1215 T)

Cat. 2.10 **GARMENT FRAGMENT**
WITH CONFRONTED STAGS
Central Asia, 7th–8th century CE

Silk samite
Length: 42 cm, width 31 cm

Inv. no. LNS 1147 T

At least six similar variants of the motif of confronted stags (sometimes identified as ibexes) are known to us. Three examples, including Cat. 2.11, feature a roundel composed of many pearls that are not divided into four regular sections. The group to which the present example belongs features roundels comprised of abutted pairs of red-and-green leaf forms evocative of the large calyces of the floral motifs that typically fill the interstices of the roundels. It is noteworthy that at the point of contact of the leaves their red extremities evoke a quatrefoil. Although this form of roundel is extremely rare, it can be seen among the textiles depicted in the Taq-i Bustan reliefs, more specifically on the trousers of a figure depicted on the large *iwan* of Khosrau II. However, in this case it does not serve to frame the main medallion with the *senmurv* motif, but instead it encloses the interstitial rosettes with deltoid-shaped leaves.[24]

The stags are rather clumsily stylized. Noticeably and for no apparent reason, their antlers are depicted in two colours. These stags, like their counterparts elsewhere, have a double row of crisscross running all the way down their fronts, and their tails are unusually long and fleshy.[25] The medallions on their abdomens are composed of two concentric circles and a gable-shaped element.

It is known from another variant of the same motif, with a blue ground and simple pearl roundels, that these textiles were used to make a cloak-like garment.[26] The Abegg Foundation holds a fragment, with its colours and texture perfectly preserved, that features a third ground colour: pale yellow.[27]

**Cat. 2.11 FRAGMENT WITH
CONFRONTED STAGS**
Central Asia, 7th–8th century CE

Silk samite
Length: 44 cm, width 10.5 cm

Inv. no. LNS 1140 T

This wedge-shaped fragment from a garment offers us a fourth ground colour: a glowing vermilion. As is the case with the fragment in the collection of the Abegg Foundation bearing a similar motif (see p. 124) the colours are perfectly preserved.[28] The stags' collars with their rows of pearls are unique to this fragment, and it is not only the branches of the antlers that are of a different colour, but also the legs and hooves. Whether this is intended to create a sense of perspective between the legs in the foreground and those at the rear can only be a matter of speculation.

The eight-pointed star and the surrounding foliate motifs between the roundels appear rather crude in comparison with the elegant foliate motifs of the previous examples.

The Abegg Foundation, which reopened to the public in 2011, possesses a magnificent garment – made all the more elegant by its back seams – that also features the same stag motif. To my knowledge, it has as yet only been published as a postcard.[29]

Detail of foliate motifs between the roundels, Cat. 2.11 (LNS 1140 T)

**Cat. 2.12 FRAGMENT WITH
PEARL ROUNDELS**
Central Asia, 7th–8th century CE

Silk samite
Length: 43 cm, width 45 cm
Literature: Zhao Feng 2007, p. 203

Inv. no. LNS 1203 T

Two well-preserved rows of pearl roundels cover this fragment of a garment. A pair of confronted stags tightly enclosed in the oval roundel stand on a split-palmette pedestal of the type found in a large number of confronted animal motifs. Once again the legs depicted in the foreground are rendered in a darker colour than the ones in the rear, and the motifs on the abdomen are similar to the ones that decorate the stags on Cat. 2.10. This stag motif is one of the most commonly found in roundels. The design lacks any special distinguishing features.

The cruciform foliate motifs between the roundels are not drawn with particular elegance.

The band of three partial roundels stitched to the right-hand edge is from the same textile, but is clearly taken from the top of a row of roundels, since the tips of some antlers are just visible.

Cat. 2.13 SILK FRAGMENT
WITH DEER MOTIFS
Central Asia,
8th–10th century CE

Silk samite
Length: 41.5 cm, width 13.5 cm

Inv. no. LNS 1200 T

Two different rows of roundels are featured on this relatively small fragment. The quadrupeds' tiny ears, stumpy horns and long tails following the upward curve of their hindquarters and terminating in perpendicular tassels suggest they are deer. Their bodies are patterned with an arbitrary arrangement of rectangles, squares and hexagons, and once again the legs in the forefront are of a different colour than those in the rear.

The deer in the upper roundel faces to the right and is set off against a red ground, and the roundel is made up of pearl motifs in two alternating colours. In the lower roundel, the deer faces in the opposite direction and is set against a pale ground, and the roundel consists of a counterchanging dotted denticulation motif. It is extremely unusual to find two different styles of roundel on the same textile.

The unusually large interstitial floral motifs appear to display a variation between their horizontal and vertical elements, and differ from the regular type of interstitial motif.

The left-hand side of this textile shows traces of a seam, once again indicating that it may have been part of a garment.

**Cat. 2.14 ROBE FRAGMENT WITH
PAIRED DUCKS IN A
PEARL ROUNDEL**
Central Asia, 7th–8th century CE

Silk samite
Length: 33 cm, width 42 cm

Inv. no. LNS 1142 T

The mandarin duck was much admired for its splendid plumage. Fortunately, the colours in this fragment have been almost perfectly preserved. The motif, which also symbolized fidelity between partners, was an especially popular subject in Sasanian textiles.

The ducks are nearly always depicted standing on a split-palmette pedestal. A red collar has here replaced the typical fluttering filets, and the traditional Sasanian pearl roundels have been turned into a scalloped floral border. The charm of these ducks lies in their well-preserved colours and steadfast pose.

**Cat. 2.15 ROUNDEL FRAGMENT
WITH DUCKS**
Central Asia, 7th–8th century CE

Silk samite
Fragment a: length 10.5 cm, width 18.5 cm
Fragment b: length 9.5 cm, width 19 cm
Assembled
fragments: 20 x 19 cm

Inv. no. LNS 1137 T a, b

This fragment features another variety of pearl roundels. Here, the original elegant row of pearl roundels is replaced by a large green band of smaller roundels, each with a pearl border of its own. The large duck in the centre of the circle has a striking blue body that helps to emphasize its dominant role, and four ducks alternate with four pheasants against a white ground in the smaller roundels.

The horizontal cut is marked by parallel traces of wear in the fabric, resulting from a seam that has been opened up. As with many other examples, we are faced with an unsolved problem – in this case, the fact that after cutting, the two pieces fit together precisely. Why the textile has been cut but none of the textile is missing remains a mystery.

Multiple variants of the pearl roundel have now been recorded; these differences may eventually enable an attempt at detailed classification, allowing the respective workshops and provenances to be established.

Cat. 2.16 FRAGMENT WITH CONFRONTED PHEASANTS
Central Asia, 8th–9th century CE

Silk samite
Length: 13 cm, width 10.5 cm

Inv. no. LNS 1139 T

Confronted birds such as pheasants, ducks and peacocks were even more common than quadruped motifs on red-ground silk samites from Central Asia. The pheasant motif reproduced here was perhaps the most popular of all. It is very similar to an example in the David Collection, Copenhagen,[30] even down to the foliate roundel composed of abutted leaf forms forming quatrefoils at their point of contact, as can been seen in Cat. 2.10.

The clear traces of seams on three sides suggest that this may have been a gusset panel.

Cat. 2.17 NARROW STRIP WITH ELONGATED BIRDS
Central Asia, 8th–9th century CE

Silk samite
Length: 38 cm, width 6 cm

Inv. no. LNS 1138 T

These distinctly elongated bird motifs – possibly doves – are oriented in opposite directions. Although there is no sign of roundels or filets, among the few details that tie this fragment to the Sasanian repertoire is the pearl collar around the bird's necks and the cup-shaped flowers that can be seen behind each bird, reminiscent of the very elegant secondary foliate motifs that we have seen on most other fragments.

Despite the major stylistic departure from the Sasanian repertoire, there is no denying the great elegance of the alternating blues and greens and the elongated form of the birds.

Cat. 2.18 FRAGMENT OF SILK SAMITE
Central Asia, 7th century CE

Silk samite
Length: 10 cm, width 21.5 cm

Inv. no. LNS 1212 T

The charm of this little fragment lies in its delicate colouring. Almost half of a floral roundel has survived, and we can see that it would have comprised sixteen petals. On a reddish-brown ground is a split-palmette pedestal upon which two pairs of feet are visible, and which probably belonged to a pair of confronted birds.

The interstitial motif consists of one half of a perfectly executed star rosette of superimposed petals, traversed by a finished edge marked by a pink line. Part of the selvedge has been preserved on the right-hand side of the fragment, and the attached remains of the original lining can be seen on the top.

Cat. 2.19 FRAGMENT WITH PAIRED GUINEA FOWL
Eastern Iran,
9th–10th century CE

Wool, woven
Resist-dyed block print
Length: 50.5 cm, width 40.2 cm
Provenance: reportedly from Samangan Province, northern Afghanistan

Inv. no. LNS 1208 T

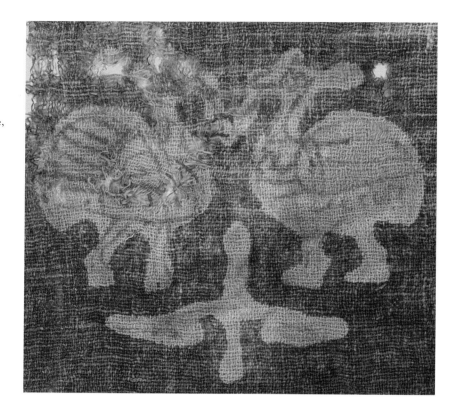

It may be assumed that the blue ground of this textile was covered with a lattice of horizontal and vertical rows of pearl roundels, although only two partial roundels have been preserved. The fragment depicts a small part of the scroll border running parallel to the right-hand selvedge.

A pair of confronted guinea fowl stands on a malformed split-palmette pedestal, their beaks connected by a filet or string of beads – a common motif in Sasanian textiles and metalwork.[31] The bodies of the guinea fowl retain clear traces of wing and feather details.

Between the roundels, the remains of an interstitial motif could represent a bird facing to the left, with its wings spread.

This resist-dyed textile is most probably a cheap block-printed version of a more expensive silk samite.

TWO EXAMPLES OF CHINESE TEXTILES

The al-Sabah Collection did not deliberately set out to collect Chinese textiles; however, as a few examples from outside of Central Asia have been acquired alongside the pieces from northern Afghanistan, they should not be overlooked.

**Cat. 2.20 TANG PERIOD SILK
WITH ROUNDELS
China, 8th–9th century CE**

Silk samite
Length: 10 cm, width 38.3 cm
One large and two smaller fragments
C-14 dating: Kiel, CE 741 ± 24 (one sigma range:
CE 776–829, 68.3%; two sigma range
CE 769–888, 95.4%)
Provenance: reportedly from Samangan Province,
northern Afghanistan

Inv. no. LNS 1178 T

This design featuring rows of roundels with foliate interstitial motifs is from the Sasanian repertoire and was emulated by China during the Tang period. The depiction of birds in flight is a popular motif often found both on Tang textiles and on contemporary silverware, but never on Sasanian or Sogdian textiles.[32]

The repetition of a cruciform plant form that fills the interstitial areas gives the "pearl" roundels a centralized focus of a kind that is not found in earlier versions. The plant forms are typically symmetrical, although they are denser and less elaborate.

The ground is now mostly brownish, but, like the wings of the birds, it was probably once red. This fragment of a garment has two vertical seams on its outer edges, and seems to have been torn off from the rest of the textile when it was recovered.

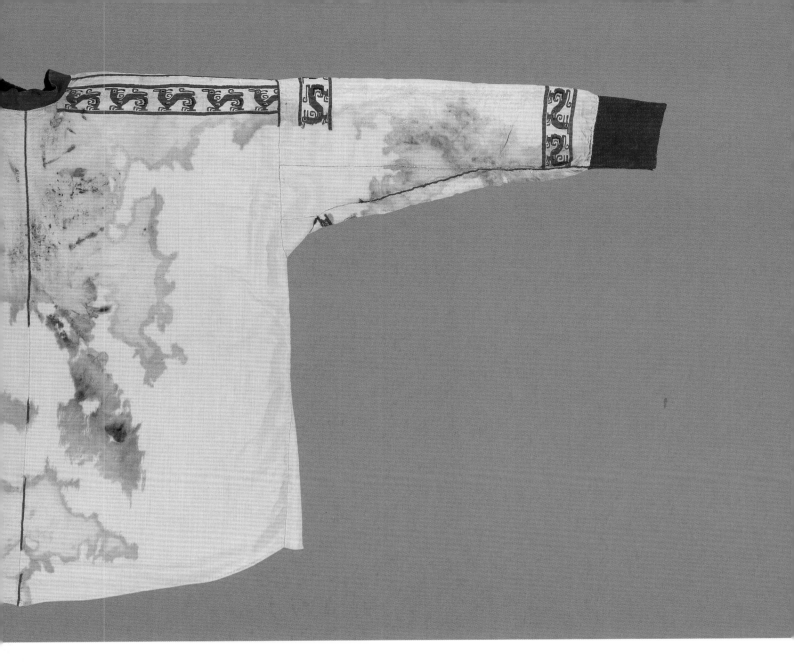

**Cat. 2.21 MAN'S JACKET WITH A
PROCESSION OF ANIMALS
China, late Han period,
early 3rd century CE**

Wool, woven
Length: 182 cm, height 80 cm
Warp: z
Weft: brown z. Red supplementary weft
pattern z.
C-14 dating: Kiel, BCE 283 ± 25 (one sigma range:
CE 264–230, 24.3%; two sigma range
CE 324–202, 73.5%)
Provenance: reportedly from Maimana, Faryab
Province, northern Afghanistan

Inv. no. LNS 1149 T

This single item of clothing from the Han period does not fit here chronologically, but there is no other suitable place for it. Among the many textiles from the eastern world in The al-Sabah Collection, this jacket is unique, and it is such a beautiful and important piece that it should not be omitted.

An identical pair of decorative bands runs across the shoulders and encircles the upper arms and cuffs. The bands are frieze-like and feature a repetition of a cherry-red winged feline or dragon regardant, with a curling tail and a snout that is slightly open. The ears, eyes, snout and the top of the fore- and hind legs are highlighted in two shades of blue and yellow. As could be seen in many examples in the Abegg Foundation exhibition of 2001 and the accompanying special edition of the *Riggisberger Berichte*, such red decorative bands were particularly popular during the Han period,[33] as was red piping.[34]

Information from the dealer gives the place of discovery as Maimana in northern Afghanistan, which is consistent with the provenances of almost all of the textiles described here.

RECENT COPIES

In East Asian art, it was considered a sign of respect to emulate the work of earlier masters and to copy their craftsmanship as closely as possible. In other words, the aim was to make copies that would be indistinguishable from the originals. Antique looms were reconstructed, so that the weaving itself was deceptively authentic.

In modern societies, famous textiles, such as the banner of Emperor Shomu now at the Shōsō-in in Nara, are copied and sold in museums in the form of scarves, tablecloths or neckties.[35] This is the same premise on which we need to base our understanding of the Sasanian silk samite copies. What is less straightforward, however, is the fact that some of these recently manufactured textiles have been given the "worn" appearance of excavated originals. Forgeries must therefore be distinguished from the originals by examination of the dye, details of the motifs and, last but not least, Carbon-14 analyses.

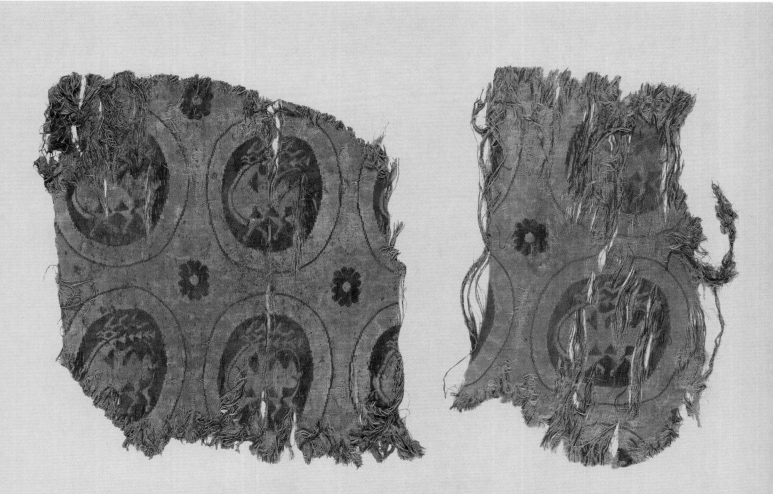

Cat. 2.22 (LNS 1150 T), fragment a

Cat. 2.22 (LNS 1150 T), fragment b

**Cat. 2.22 TEXTILE FRAGMENTS WITH
A PROCESSION OF STAGS**
China (?), modern

Silk, very heavy uneven weave
Fragment a: length 33 cm, width 37 cm
Fragment b: length 23 cm, width 41 cm
Fragment c: length 22 cm, width 43 cm
Fragment d: length 28.5 cm, width 40 cm
C-14 dating: Kiel, recent, *c.* 1954 CE
Provenance: reportedly from Samangan Province,
northern Afghanistan

Inv. no. LNS 1150 T a–d

On the development and distribution of this stag motif, see the accounts given by Zhao Feng.[36]

The stags here are rather clumsily executed, and depicted in almost caricatural manner. The colours are dull, pallid and unattractive. This is not a respectful homage but a corrupted copy in which not even the alternating direction of the rows of stags has been accurately rendered.

The adulterated signs of wear are crude and, worse still, illogical. Where this unusually thick, coarse textile was woven remains unknown.

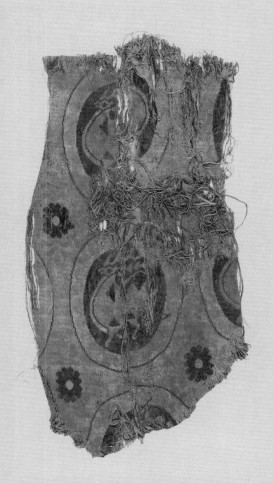

Cat. 2.22 (LNS 1150 T), fragment c

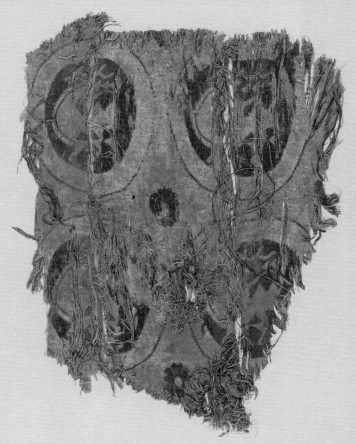

Cat. 2.22 (LNS 1150 T), fragment d

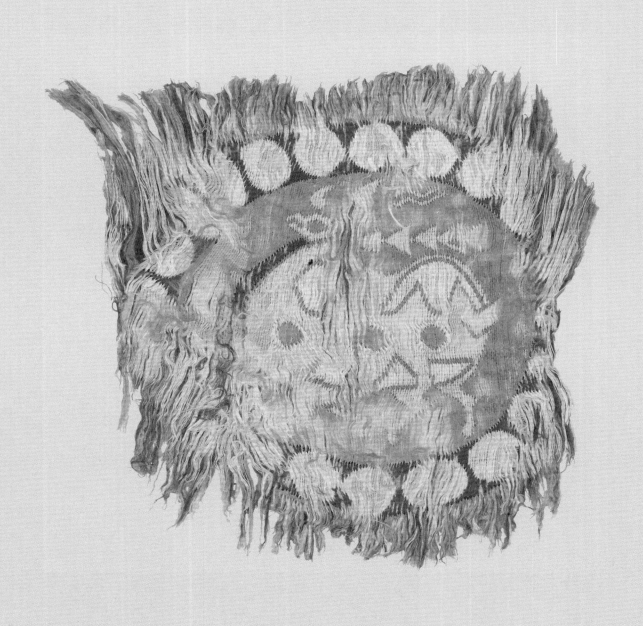

Cat. 2.23 ROUNDEL WITH STAG
China (?), modern

Silk
Length: 16 cm, width 16 cm

Inv. no. LNS 1169 T

The similarity between this stag and the rendering of stags on the previous example, as well as the use of two almost certainly synthetic dyes – the bright turquoise roundels and the faded orange patches on the stag's body – are so obvious that anyone with a sense of what constitutes art and colour can discern with the naked eye that this is a forgery.

SHARED MOTIFS IN PRE-ISLAMIC TEXTILES

The most striking stylistic feature of this post-Sasanian group of Central Asian textiles is its strict adherence to a particular style of silhouetted animal motif. Even birds are shown in statuesque poses, never in flight.

Chinese artists, on the other hand, constantly strove to portray movement in their motifs of birds, dragons and mythological creatures such as winged horses.

Landscapes and seascapes are not featured.

Another striking feature is the fact that the animals are not shown with realistic skin or feather patterns. Instead, the artists preferred to use stylized interpretations to indicate feathers on the ducks (Cat. 2.14 and Cat. 2.15), feathers on the elongated birds (Cat. 2.17), and fleece on the rams (Cat. 2.5 and Cat. 2.13).

Among the nineteen different examples from the al-Sabah Collection, seven different types of pearl roundel can be distinguished.

Cat 2.9 (LNS 1215 T)

Cat 2.2 (LNS 1145 T)

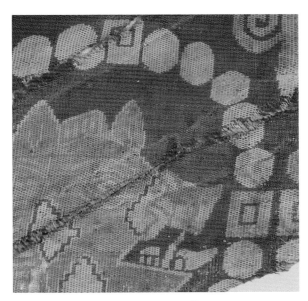

Cat 2.6 (LNS 1136 T)

Cat 2.8 (LNS 1201 T)

Cat 2.10 (LNS 1147 T)

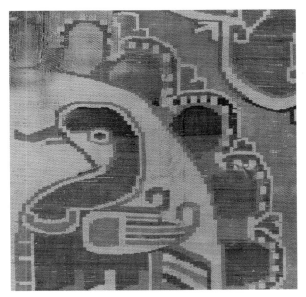

Cat 2.14 (LNS 1142 T)

Cat 2.15 (LNS 1137 T), fragments a, b

CARBON-14 DATING INFORMATION

CAT. NUMBER	INV. NUMBER	LABORATORY	DATE OF ANALYSIS	SAMPLE NUMBER	CONVENTIONAL AGE (BP = Before Present, present being 1950)	CORRECTED DATE	δ13C %	CALIBRATED AGE RANGES
1.1–1.2	LNS 47 R a–g only fragment "a" tested	Research Laboratory for Archaeology and the History of Art, Oxford, UK	Jul 1988	OXA7610	BP 1725 ± 40	CE 225 ± 40	-19.27	(two sigma range: CE 220–410) CE 410
1.3	LNS 47 R h	Institute for Particle Physics, Zürich, Switzerland	Jan 2000	ETH21264	BP 1810 ± 50	CE 140 ± 50	-17.5 ± 1.1	(two sigma range: CE 114–348)
1.4	LNS 64 R	Research Laboratory for Archaeology and the History of Art, Oxford, UK	Oct 2006	OXA16406	BP 1793 ± 28	CE 157 ± 28	-21.0	(one sigma range: CE 130–260, 57.9%; two sigma range: CE 130–270, 77.8%)
1.5	LNS 53 R	Research Laboratory for Archaeology and the History of Art, Oxford, UK	Oct 2006	OXA16396	BP 1732 ± 27	CE 218 ± 27	-19.6	(one sigma range: CE 250–345, 68.2%; two sigma range: CE 240–390, 95.4%)
1.6	LNS 51 R	Institute for Particle Physics, Zürich, Switzerland	Jan 2000	ETH21266	BP 1600 ± 50	CE 350 ± 50	-16.1 ± 1.1	(two sigma range: CE 378–598)
1.7	LNS 73 R	Leibniz Laboratory for Radiometric Dating and Isotopic Research, Kiel, Germany	Aug 2010	KIA43224	BP 1640 ± 30	CE 310 ± 30	-18.63 ± 0.14	(one sigma range: CE 351–367, 56.7%; two sigma range: CE 336–468, 79.2%)
1.8	LNS 74 R	Leibniz Laboratory for Radiometric Dating and Isotopic Research, Kiel, Germany	Aug 2010	KIA43225	BP 1660 ± 25	CE 290 ± 25	-21.49 ± 0.78	(one sigma range: CE 381–420, 58.1%; two sigma range: CE 332–430, 93.5%)
1.9	LNS 67 R a–h only fragment "a" tested	Research Laboratory for Archaeology and the History of Art, Oxford, UK	Oct 2006	OXA16408	BP 1612 ± 28	CE 338 ± 28	-19.6	(one sigma range: CE 400–440, 29.8%: two sigma range: CE 390–540, 95.4%)
1.10	LNS 63 R	Research Laboratory for Archaeology and the History of Art, Oxford, UK	Oct 2006	OXA16405	BP 1621 ± 27	CE 329 ± 27	-21.3	(one sigma range: CE 390–440, 39.6%; two sigma range: CE 380–540, 95.4%)
1.11	LNS 70 R	Leibniz Laboratory for Radiometric Dating and Isotopic Research, Kiel, Germany	Aug 2009	KIA39131	BP 1513 ± 23	CE 437 ± 23	-22.28 ± 0.27	(one sigma range: CE 540–585, 66.3%)
1.12	LNS 71 R a–c only fragment "a" tested	Leibniz Laboratory for Radiometric Dating and Isotopic Research, Kiel, Germany	Aug 2009	KIA39132	BP 1482 ± 27	CE 468 ± 27	-22.01 ± 0.29	(one sigma range: CE 558–609, 68.3%; two sigma range: CE 543–638, 95.4%)
1.13	LNS 62 R a–c only fragment "a" tested	IsoTrace Laboratory, The Canadian Centre for Accelerator Mass Spectometry, University of Toronto, Canada	Mar 2001	TO9534	BP 1530 ± 50	CE 420 ± 50	-25	(one sigma range weft; CE 415–535, 68.3%; two sigma range weft: CE 415–640, 95.5%; one sigma range pile; CE 525–600, 68.3%; two sigma pile; CE 415–640, 95.5%)

CAT. NUMBER	INV. NUMBER	LABORATORY	DATE OF ANALYSIS	SAMPLE NUMBER	CONVENTIONAL AGE (BP = Before Present, present being 1950)	CORRECTED DATE	δ13C %	CALIBRATED AGE RANGES
1.14	LNS 48 R a–e only fragment "a" tested	Research Laboratory for Archaeology and the History of Art, Oxford, UK	Jul 1998	OXA7611	BP 1480 ± 35	CE 470 ± 35	-21.02	(one sigma range: CE 545–620, 68.2%; two sigma range: CE 450–650, 95.4%)
1.14	LNS 48 R a–e only fragment "a" tested	Institute for Particle Physics, Zürich, Switzerland	Jan 2000	ETH21265	BP 1445 ± 50	CE 505 ± 50	-17.6 ± 1.1	(two sigma range: CE 535–680, 100%)
1.15	LNS 61 R only fragment "f" tested	Research Laboratory for Archaeology and the History of Art, Oxford, UK	Oct 2006	OXA16404	BP 1464 ± 27	CE 486 ± 27	-21.1	(one sigma range: CE 595–645, 68.2%; two sigma range: CE 565–655, 95.4%)
1.17	LNS 1085 T	IsoTrace Laboratory, The Canadian Centre for Accelerator Mass Spectometry, University of Toronto, Canada	Apr 2001	TO9535	BP 1430 ± 60	CE 520 ± 60	-25	(one sigma range: CE 595–660, 68.3%; two sigma range: CE 535–685, 95.5%)
1.18	LNS 72 R	Leibniz Laboratory for Radiometric Dating and Isotopic Research, Kiel, Germany	Aug 2010	KIA43223	BP 957 ± 25	CE 993 ± 25	-20.50 ± 0.13	(one sigma range: CE 1088–1122, 34.5%; two sigma range: CE 1075–1154, 63.9%)
1.19	LNS 78 R	RCD Lockinge: Tritium & Carbon-14 Analysis and Consultancy, East Lockinge, Oxfordshire, UK	Nov 2010	RCD-7543	BP 1370 ± 40	CE 580 ± 40	N/A	(one sigma range: CE 640–688, 68%; two sigma range: CE 600–720, 95%)
1.20	LNS 56 R	Research Laboratory for Archaeology and the History of Art, Oxford, UK	Oct 2006	OXA16399	BP 1446 ± 27	CE 504 ± 27	-19.8	(one sigma range: CE 595–645, 68.2%; two sigma range: CE 565–655, 95.4%)
1.21	LNS 58 R a–b only fragment "a" tested	Research Laboratory for Archaeology and the History of Art, Oxford, UK	Oct 2006	OXA16401	BP 970 ± 27	CE 980 ± 27	-21.2	(one sigma range: CE 1020–1050, 30.5%; one sigma range: CE 1090–1150, 37.7%; two sigma range: CE 1010–1160, 95.4%)
1.22	LNS 54 R	Research Laboratory for Archaeology and the History of Art, Oxford, UK	Oct 2006	OXA16397	BP 861 ± 26	CE 1089 ± 26	-22.2	(one sigma range: CE 1160–1215, 68.2%; two sigma range: CE 1150–1260, 86.1%)
1.23	LNS 55 R a–c	Research Laboratory for Archaeology and the History of Art, Oxford, UK	Oct 2006	OXA16398	BP 1188 ± 28	CE 762 ± 28	-21.3	(one sigma range: CE 800–890, 61.0%; two sigma range: CE 770–900, 90.2%)
1.24	LNS 66 R	Research Laboratory for Archaeology and the History of Art, Oxford, UK	Oct 2006	OXA16407	BP 1104 ± 27 years	CE 846 ± 27	-20.4	(one sigma range: CE 940–980, 41.2%; two sigma range: CE 880–1020, 95.4%)
1.25	LNS 69 R	Leibniz Laboratory for Radiometric Dating and Isotopic Research, Kiel, Germany	Jun 2007	KIA33010	BP 924 ± 26	CE 1026 ± 27	-18.73 ± 0.37	(textile fibres, alkali residue 4.0 mg C 925 ± 25 BP; textile fibres, acid residue 3.0 mg C 910 ± 25 BP)

CAT. NUMBER	INV. NUMBER	LABORATORY	DATE OF ANALYSIS	SAMPLE NUMBER	CONVENTIONAL AGE (BP = Before Present, present being 1950)	CORRECTED DATE	δ13C %	CALIBRATED AGE RANGES
1.26	LNS 59 R	Research Laboratory for Archaeology and the History of Art, Oxford, UK	Oct 2006	OXA16402	BP 844 ± 26 years	CE 1106 ± 26	-21.6	(one sigma range: CE 1165–1225, 68.2%; two sigma range: CE 1150–1270, 95.4%)
1.27	LNS 60 R	Research Laboratory for Archaeology and the History of Art, Oxford, UK	Oct 2006	OXA16403	BP 819 ± 26	CE 1131 ± 26	-21.3	(one sigma range: CE 1205–1260, 68.2%; two sigma range: CE 1150–1270, 95.4%)
2.1	LNS 1144 T a	Leibniz Laboratory for Radiometric Dating and Isotopic Research, Kiel, Germany	Jun 2007	KIA33013	BP 1395 ± 25	CE 555 ± 25	-20.75 ± 0.09	(one sigma range: CE 639–663, 64.2%)
2.2	LNS 1145 T a	Leibniz Laboratory for Radiometric Dating and Isotopic Research, Kiel, Germany	Jun 2007	KIA33014	BP 1455 ± 25	CE 495 ± 25	-20.26 ± 0.12	(one sigma range: CE 597–643, 65.6%; two sigma range: 558–651, 94.4%)
2.3	LNS 1174 T	Leibniz Laboratory for Radiometric Dating and Isotopic Research, Kiel, Germany	Feb 2009	KIA38108	BP 1445 ± 25	CE 505 ± 25	-23.62 ± 0.36	(one sigma range: CE 601–642, 68.3%; two sigma range: CE 571–650, 95.4%)
2.4	LNS 548 T	Institute for Particle Physics, Zürich, Switzerland	Jan 2000	ETH21243	BP 1515 ± 45	CE 435 ± 45	-19.4 ± 1.1	
2.5	LNS 1143 T a	Leibniz Laboratory for Radiometric Dating and Isotopic Research, Kiel, Germany	Jun 2007	KIA33012	BP 1565 ± 28	CE 385 ± 28	-21.17 ± 0.13	(one sigma range: CE 462–522, 49.2%; two sigma range: CE 423–545, 91.6%)
2.7	LNS 1175 T	Leibniz Laboratory for Radiometric Dating and Isotopic Research, Kiel, Germany	Feb 2009	KIA38109	BP 1485 ± 25	CE 465 ± 25	-21.61 ± 0.29	(one sigma range: CE 558–605, 68.3%; two sigma range: CE 542–635, 95.4%)
2.20	LNS 1178 T	Leibniz Laboratory for Radiometric Dating and Isotopic Research, Kiel, Germany	Feb 2009	KIA38110	BP 1209 ± 24	CE 741 ± 24	-22.44 ± 0.10	(one sigma range: CE 776–829, 68.3%; two sigma range: CE 769–888, 95.4%)
2.21	LNS 1149 T	Leibniz Laboratory for Radiometric Dating and Isotopic Research, Kiel, Germany	Jun 2007	KIA33016	BP 2233 ± 25	BCE 283 ± 25	-16.88 ± 0.16	(one sigma range: CE 264–230, 24.3%; two sigma range: CE 324–202, 73.5%)
2.22	LNS 1150 T a	Leibniz Laboratory for Radiometric Dating and Isotopic Research, Kiel, Germany		KIA33017	BP > 1954		-24.95 ± 0.19	

RADIOCARBON DATING USING ACCELERATED MASS SPECTROMETRY

The method of radiocarbon dating is based on the fact that all living organisms are constantly exchanging carbon atoms with their environment. These atoms include the main stable isotope (12C) and an unstable isotope (14C). When an organism dies, it contains a measurable ratio of 14C to 12C, and, as the 14C decays with no possibility of replenishment, the ratio decreases at a regular rate (the half-life of 14C). It is the measurement of 14C decay that can provide an indication of the age of any carbon-based material.

When interpreting a radiocarbon date such as 1155 ± 25 BP the mathematics will be 1950 minus 1155 which equals 795 plus or minus 25 – which gives a corrected date of CE 795 ± 25.

Radiocarbon dating is only able to give approximate dates and its results, therefore, are given in units of mean and standard deviations, which are known as sigmas. The two sigma ranges used in the analyses represent the statistical range in which the mean date may fall. The first sigma is the time span that radiocarbon dating theory suggests would contain the actual date 68% of the time; and the second sigma is a wider time span that would theoretically include the date 98% of the time.

Where it comes to analysing the results of carbon testing, it should be observed that these sigmas or date ranges are not narrow. Where the first sigma is concerned, the time span can range to over a hundred years. When the second sigma is taken into consideration, this time span can extend to well over two hundred years.

Radiocarbon dating can therefore only give us a supposed date range of the age of an object. This does not necessarily indicate the date at which an object is produced; rather, as in the case of a wool carpet, dating can indicate when the wool was produced.

The abbreviation BP is short for 'Before Present', and the given date for 'Present' is 1950, a convention that honours the first calibrations and publication of radiocarbon dates in December of 1950.

Sophie C. Budden
Head of Conservation,
The al-Sabah Collection

NOTES

INTRODUCTION

1 Spuhler 2012, pp. 15–21.
2 When interpreting a radiocarbon date such as 1155 ± 25 BP (Before Present) the mathematics will be 1950 minus 1155 which equals 795 plus or minus 25 – which gives a corrected date of CE 795 ± 25. Radiocarbon dating is only able to give approximate dates and its results, therefore, are given in units of mean and standard deviations, which are known as sigmas. The two sigma ranges given in the catalogue entries represent the statistical range in which the mean date may fall. The first sigma is the timespan that radiocarbon dating theory suggests would contain the actual date 68% of the time; and the second sigma is a wider timespan that would theoretically include the date 98% of the time.
3 Splendeur Cat. 1993, pl. 129.
4 Lessing 1900–9; Flemming 1927, pp. 20–22.

PART 1: CARPETS FROM THE SASANIAN PERIOD

1 Rudenko 1970, pp. 174–75.
2 Gantzhorn 1990, p. 50.
3 Whitfield / Ferrer 1990, p. 121, no. 95.
4 Erdmann 1943, p. 121ff; Pope / Ackermann 1938–39, p. 681ff.
5 Samangan, known in ancient times as Eukratidia, is the name of a town and a province in northern Afghanistan (36.15° N–68.1° E). It was well known as a centre of Buddhism in the fourth to fifth centuries CE. Numerous caves carved into the rocks were used as shelters.
6 On cave burials, see Splendeur Cat. 1993, pp. 41–42.
7 The institutions that have carried out the Carbon-14 dating for this book are: a) Institute for Particle Physics, Zürich, Switzerland [hereafter referred to as: Zürich]; b) Leibniz Laboratory for Radiometric Dating and Isotopic Research, Kiel, Germany [hereafter referred to as: Kiel]; c) Research Laboratory for Archaeology and the History of Art, Oxford, England [hereafter referred to as: Oxford]; d) IsoTrace Laboratory, the Canadian Centre for Accelerator Mass Spectometry, University of Toronto, Canada [hereafter referred to as: Toronto]; e) RCD Lockinge: Tritium & Carbon-14 Analysis and Consultancy, East Lockinge, Oxfordshire, UK [hereafter referred to as: Oxfordshire].

Depictions of Sasanian Carpets

8 Belenizki 1980, pp. 11, 14 and 85, among others.
9 Ibid., p. 82, room VI/1.
10 Marshak 1986, p. 50 and ills 30 and 32 (detail).
11 Trever / Lukonin 1987, ills 18–19, 29–30; Marshak 1986, ill. 33; Ghirshman 1962, p. 218.

Cat. 1.1

12 Riggisberger Berichte 10 (2001).

Cat. 1.7

13 Sarre 1923, pls 39–41.
14 Stawinski 1979, pl. 128. Here he reproduces a Kushan-Bactrian capital from Karatepe (2nd–4th century) that features a similar cat-like head, which he describes as a griffin.
15 Trever / Lukonin 1987, fig. 106.

Cat. 1.8

16 Trever / Lukonin 1987, pls 71, 72, 86 and 87.

Cat. 1.13

17 Boris Marshak, in oral communication with the author.
18 See, for example, the Sasanian stucco tile in the Museum of Islamic Art in Berlin that portrays a ram in the same posture, Museum of Islamic Art, Berlin, Inv. no. I 2212.
19 Fukai 1969, vol. 1, pl. XXXII.

Sasanian Flatweaves

20 ICOC San Francisco 1990.
21 Hali 59 (October 1991), pp. 95–99.
22 Pope / Ackermann 1938–39, pls 211, 213, 214 and 218; Marshak 1986, nos 3, 4, 6, 8 and 183.
23 Pope / Ackermann 1938–39, pls 230 A and B; Trever / Lukonin 1987, pls 18, 19, 23, 25, 33 and 34.

Cat. 1.17

24 See Trever / Lukonin 1987, nos 8, 15 and 16.

Cat. 1.19

25 See Trever / Lukonin 1987, pls 8, 30 and 33.

Cat. 1.20

26 Dimand / Mailey 1973, fig. 21.

Cat. 1.21

27 "Offset knotting" is a technique in which knots are staggered across warp bundles from row to row.

Cat. 1.22

28 See, for example, Erdmann 1966, fig. 159.

Cat. 1.24

29 Hamilton 1959, pls XLVIII, 3 and XLIX.

PART 2: SASANIAN AND SOGDIAN TEXTILES

1 Sarre 1923, pp. 100–1; Pope / Ackermann 1938–39, pl. 983A; Erdmann 1943, ills 96B–100.
2 Fukai 1969.
3 Watt / Wardwell 1998, p. 23.
4 Otavsky 1998.
5 Hali 145–48 (2006), pp. 170–75.
6 Kirchenschätze: Falke 1913, vol. II, nos 235 and 241.
7 Natschläger 1984.
8 Zhao Feng 2002 and Zhao Feng 1999.
9 Watt / Wardwell 1998.

Textiles from The al-Sabah Collection and their iconography

10 The outstanding examples in the Abegg Foundation in Riggisberg, near Berne, have to my knowledge only been published in part (Riggisberger Berichte 1998 and 2006; and Otavsky / Wardwell 2011).
11 Splendeur Cat. 1993, nos 3–13.
12 Trever / Lukonin 1987, pls 60 (centre), 73, 83, 98 and 112.
13 Splendeur Cat. 1993, nos 147–61.
14 Zhao Feng 1999, p. 121.
15 Splendeur Cat. 1993, pl. 4.

Cat. 2.1

16 Falke 1913, vol. I, fig. 110; Natschläger 1984, p. 97; Splendeur Cat. 1993, fig. 131, p. 136.

Cat. 2.5

17 Martiniani-Reber 1986, no. 10, p. 44.
18 Hali 151 (Spring 2007), p. 88, ill. 7 (Carbon-14 dating: 1593 ± 25 years BP).
19 Another example is in the collection of the Abegg Foundation, Riggisberg (Inv. no. 5432).

Cat. 2.8

20 Jerusalimskaja 1996, pls LXXIII and LXXIV.
21 Lucidi Cat. 1994, cats. 25, 33 and 31.

Cat. 2.9

22 Falke 1913, vol. II, figs 24 and 237.
23 The David Collection, Copenhagen (recent acquisition; unpublished).

Cat. 2.10

24 Fukai 1969, vol. I, pl. XLVII and preceding plates.
25 Hali 140 (May–June 2005), p. 117, ill. 4.
26 Hali 138, January–February 2005, p. 85, ill. 1; and Hali 151, Spring 2007, p. 89, ill. 9 (caption 10); Katoen Natie Collection, Antwerp.
27 Riggisberger Berichte 6, 1998, p. 20, ill. 4.

Cat. 2.11

28 Riggisberger Berichte 6, 1998, p. 20, ill. 4.
29 Abegg Foundation, Inv. no. 5405/5409.

Cat. 2.16

30 Folsach 2001, ill. 622.

Cat. 2.19

31 Splendeur Cat. 1993, pl. 47, p. 186.

Cat. 2.20

32 Watt / Wardwell 1998, pl. 20.

Cat. 2.21

33 Riggisberger Berichte 10 (2001), figs 35 and 95.
34 Ibid., figs 15 and 17.

Recent copies

35 As, for example, at the Tokyo National Museum.

Cat. 2.22

36 Zhao Feng 1999, ill. p. 96, text p. 97; and another example illustrated in Cultural Relics Unearthed in Sinkiang, Museum of the Sinkiang Uighur Autonomous Region, Beijing, 1975, p. 100.

BIBLIOGRAPHY

Ackerman 1953
Ackerman, Phyllis, "Persian Textiles",
Ciba Review 98 (1953), p. 3506

Anon. 1991
"Early Iranian Textiles from Shahr-I-Qumis",
Hali 59 (1991), pp. 95–99

Arizzoli-Clémentel 1990
Arizzoli-Clémentel, Pierre, *Le Musée des Tissus de
Lyon* (Paris, 1990)

Belenizki 1980
Belenizki, A. M., *Mittelasien: Kunst der Sogden*
(Leipzig, 1980)

Bénazeth / Martiniani-Reber 1997
Bénazeth, Dominique, and Marielle Martiniani-
Reber, preface by Christiane Ziegler, *Textiles et
Mode Sassanides: les Tissus Orientaux Conservés au
Département des Antiquités Égyptiennes* (Paris, 1997)

Binyon / Wilkinson / Gray 1933
Binyon, Laurence, J. V. S. Wilkinson and Basil Gray,
Persian Miniature Painting (London, 1933)

Blair / Bloom / Wardwell 1993
Blair, Sheila, Jonathan Bloom and Anne Wardwell,
"Reevaluating the date of the 'Buyid' silks by epigraphic
and radiocarbon analysis", *Ars Orientalis* 22 (1992),
pp. 1–41

Bouvier Cat. 1993
*Tissus d'Égypte. Témoins du Monde Arabe VIIIe–XVe
siècles: Collection Bouvier* (Paris and Geneva, 1993)

Carboni 1995
Carboni, Stefano, in Juri A. Petrosjan et al. (eds),
*Von Bagdad bis Isfahan: Buchmalerei und Schriftkunst
des Vorderen Orients (8.–18. Jh.) aus dem Institut für
Orientalistik, St. Petersburg* (Lugano, 1995), p. 152ff

Carter / Goldstein 2013
Carter, Martha, and Sidney Goldstein, *Splendors of the
Ancient East: Antiquities from The al-Sabah Collection*
(London, 2013)

Cornu / Martiniani-Reber / Fiette 2008
Cornu, Georgette, Marielle Martiniani-Reber and
Alexandre Fiette, *Tissus Islamiques: Collections du
Musée d'Art et d'Histoire de Genève* (Geneva, 2008)

Curatola / Keene /Kaoukji 2010
Curatola, Giovanni, Manuel Keene and Salam Kaoukji,
Al-Fann: Art from the Islamic Civilization (Milan, 2010)

Dimand / Mailey 1973
Dimand, Maurice S., and Jean Mailey, *Oriental Rugs in
the Metropolitan Museum of Art* (New York, 1973)

Erdmann 1943
Erdmann, Kurt, *Die Kunst Irans zur Zeit der Sasaniden*
(Leipzig, 1943)

Erdmann 1966
Erdmann, Kurt, *Siebenhundert Jahre Orientteppich:
Zu seiner Geschichte und Erforschung*, Hanna Erdmann
(ed.) (Herford, 1966)

Errera 1927
Errera, Isabelle, *Catalogue d'Étoffes Anciennes et
Modernes* (Brussels, 1927)

Ettinghausen 1959
Ettinghausen, Richard, *Aus der Welt der islamischen
Kunst: Festschrift für Ernst Kühnel zum 75. Geburtstag
am 26. 10. 1957* (Berlin, 1959)

Ettinghausen 1962
Ettinghausen, Richard, *Arabische Malerei* (Geneva, 1962)

Ettinghausen 1972
Ettinghausen, Richard, *From Byzantium to Sasanian
Iran and the Islamic World* (Leiden, 1972)

Falke 1913
Falke, Otto von, *Kunstgeschichte der Seidenweberei*,
2 vols (Berlin, 1913)

Feltham 2010
Feltham, Heleanor B., *Lions, Silks and Silver:
The influence of Sasanian Persia*, Sino-Platonic Papers
206 (Philadelphia, 2010)

Flemming 1927
Flemming, Ernst, *Das Textilwerk* (Berlin, 1927)

Folsach / Bernsted 1993
Folsach, Kjeld von, and Anne-Marie Keblow Bernsted,
Woven Treasures: Textiles from the World of Islam
(Copenhagen, 1993)

Folsach 2001
Folsach, Kjeld von, *Art from the World of Islam in the
David Collection* (Copenhagen, 2001)

Fukai 1969
Fukai, Shinji, *Taq-i-Bustan, The Tokyo University
Iraq-Iran Archaeological Expedition*, 2 vols (Tokyo, 1969)

Galloway 2000
Galloway, Francesca, *Asian Textiles, Indian Miniatures
& Works of Art 2000* (London, 2000)

Gantzhorn 1990
Gantzhorn, Volkmar, *Der christlich-orientalische
Teppich* (Cologne, 1990)

Gao Hanyu 1987 and 1992
Gao Hanyu, foreword by Krishna Riboud, *Soieries
de Chine* (Paris, 1987); tr. as *Chinese Textile Designs*,
Rosemary Scott and Susan Whitfield (London, 1992)

Ghirshman 1962
Ghirshman, Roman, *Iran: Parther und Sasaniden*
(Munich, 1962)

Grube 1968
Grube, Ernst, *The Classical Style in Islamic Painting*
(Venice, 1968)

Haase 2007
Haase, Claus-Peter (ed.), *Sammlerglück: Islamische
Kunst aus der Sammlung Edmund de Unger*
(Munich, 2007)

Hali
*Hali: The International Journal of Oriental Carpets
and Textiles / Die internationale Zeitschrift für
Orientteppiche und Textilien* (London, 1978–)

Hall 2006
Hall, Chris (ed.), *Power Dressing: Textiles for Rulers and
Priests from the Chris Hall Collection* (Singapore, 2006)

Hamilton 1959
Hamilton, Robert W., *Khirbat al-Mafjar: An Arabian
Mansion in the Jordan Valley* (Oxford, 1959)

Harper 1978
Harper, Prudence Oliver, *The Royal Hunter:
Art of the Sasanian Empire* (New York, 1978)

Helmecke 2001
Helmecke, G., *Byzantinische und orientalische
Seidenstoffe: Grabfunde aus der Sepultur der
Bamberger Domherren* (Bamberg, 2001)

Irwin / Hall 1971
Irwin, John, and Margaret Hall, *Indian Painted
and Printed Fabrics* (Bombay, 1971)

Jerusalimskaja 1996
Jerusalimskaja, Anna, *Die Gräber der Moscevaja Balka:
Frühmittelalterliche Funde an der nordkaukasischen
Seidenstraße* (Munich, 1996)

Kageyama 2003
Kageyama, Etsuko, "Use and production of silks in
Sogdiana", *Ērān ud Anērān, Webfestschrift Marshak*
(2003)

Kawami 1992
Kawami, Trudy S., "Archaeological Evidence for Textiles
in Pre-Islamic Iran", *Iranian Studies* 25, 1–2 (1992),
pp. 7–18

Kendrick 1924
Kendrick, Albert Frank, *Catalogue of Muhammadan
Textiles of the Medieval Period* (London, 1924)

King 1987
King, Donald, "The Textiles found near Rayy about
1925", *Bulletin de Liaison du Centre International
d'Étude des Textiles Anciens* 65 (1987), pp. 34–59

Krahl 1989
Krahl, Regina, "Designs on Early Chinese Textiles",
Orientations 20/8 (1989), pp. 62–73

Kröger 1982
Kröger, Jens, *Sasanidischer Stuckdekor* (Mainz, 1982)

Kühnel 1922
Kühnel, Ernst, *Miniaturmalerei im Islamischen Orient*
(Berlin, 1922)

Kühnel 1927
Kühnel, Ernst, *Islamische Stoffe aus ägyptischen
Gräbern in der islamischen Kunstabteilung und
in der Stoffsammlung des Schlossmuseums*
(Berlin, 1927)

Lamm 1937
Lamm, Carl Johan, *Cotton in Mediaeval Textiles of
the Near East* (Paris, 1937)

Lentz / Lowry 1989
Lentz, Thomas W., and Glenn D. Lowry, *Timur and
the Princely Vision: Persian Art and Culture in the
Fifteenth Century* (Los Angeles, 1989)

Lessing 1900–9
Lessing, Julius, *Königliche Museen Berlin: Die Gewebe-
Sammlung des Kunstgewerbe-Museums*, 11 vols
(Berlin, 1900–9)

Lucidi Cat. 1994
Lucidi, Maria Teresa (ed.), *La seta e la sua via*
(Rome, 1994)

Mackie 1984
Mackie, Louise, "Toward an Understanding of Mamluk
Silks: National and International Considerations",
Muqarnas, vol. 2 (1984), pp. 127–46

Marshak 1986
Marshak, Boris, *Silberschätze des Orients: Metallkunst
des 3.–13. Jahrhunderts und ihre Kontinuität*
(Leipzig, 1986)

Martiniani-Reber 1986
Martiniani-Reber, Marielle, *Lyon, Musée Historique
des Tissues: Soieries Sassanides, Coptes et Byzantines
Ve–XIe siècle* (Paris, 1986)

May 1957
    May, Florence Lewis, *Silk Textiles of Spain*
    (New York, 1957)

Meissner 1988
    Meissner, Marek, *Das Goldene Zeitalter Arabiens
    Unter den Abbasiden* (Hanau, 1988)

Miao Liangyun 1988
    Miao Liangyun, *China's Silk Patterns through the Ages*
    (Beijing, 1988)

Migeon 1929
    Migeon, Gaston, *Les Arts du Tissu* (Paris, 1929)

Muthesius 1997
    Muthesius, Anna, *Byzantine Silk Weaving:
    AD 400 to AD 1200 Byzantinische Gechichtsschreiber /
    Ergänzungsband 4* (Vienna, 1997)

Natschläger 1984
    Natschläger, Helga, *Zu einigen in Turfan Astana
    ausgegrabenen polychromen Seidengeweben des 3. bis
    8. Jh. n. Chr.*, [unpublished dissertation] (Vienna, 1984)

Ogasawara 1989
    Ogasawara, Sae, "Chinese Fabrics of the Song and
    Yuan Dynasties Preserved in Japan", *Orientations*,
    20/8 (1989), pp. 32–44

Otavsky / Abbas 1995
    Otavsky, Karel, and Muhammad Abbas, *Mittelalterliche
    Textilien I: Ägypten, Persien und Mesopotamien,
    Spanien und Nordafrika* (Riggisberg, 1995)

Otavsky 1998
    Otavsky, Karl, "Zur kunsthistorischen Einordnung der
    Stoffe", *Entlang der Seidenstrasse: Frümittelalterliche
    Kunst zwischen Persien und China in der Abegg-
    Stiftung*, Karl Otavsky (ed.) *Riggisberger Berichte 6*
    (1988), pp. 119–214

Otavsky / Wardwell 2011
    Otavsky, Karel, and Anne E. Wardwell, *Mittelalterliche
    Textilien II, Zwischen Europa und China*
    (Riggisberg, 2011)

Petsopoulos 1979
    Petsopoulos, Yanni, *Kilims: The Art of Tapestry
    Weaving in Anatolia, the Caucasus and Persia*
    (London, 1979)

Pfister 1938
    Pfister, Rodolphe, *Les Toiles Imprimées de Fostat
    et l'Hindoustan* (Paris, 1938)

Phipps 2010
    Phipps, Elena, "Cochineal Red: The Art History
    of a Color", *Metropolitan Museum of Art Bulletin*,
    67/3 (2010)

Piotrovsky 1993
    Piotrovsky, Mikhail, *Lost Empire of the Silk Road:
    Buddhist Art from Khara Khoto (X–XIIIth century)*
    (Milan, 1993)

Polosmak / Barkova 2005
    Polosmak, N. V., and L. L. Barkova, *Kostjum i Tekstil
    pasyrykzev Altaja* (Novosibirsk, 2005)

Pope / Ackermann 1938–39
    Pope, Arthur Upham, and Phyllis Ackermann,
    *A Survey of Persian Art from Prehistoric Times to
    the Present*, 6 vols (London and New York 1938–39;
    repr. in 12 vols, 1967)

Riboud / Vial 1970
    Riboud, Krishna, and Gabriel Vial, *Tissus de
    Touen-Houang Conservés au Musée Guimet et à
    la Bibliothèque Nationale.* Mission Paul Pelliot,
    Documents Archéologiques 13 (Paris, 1970)

Rice / Gray 1976
    Rice, David Talbot and Basil Gray (ed.), *Illustrations to
    the 'World History' of Rashid al-Din* (Edinburgh, 1976)

Riggisberger Berichte
    Riggisberger Berichte (Riggisberg, 1993–)

Rudenko 1968
    Rudenko, Sergei I., *Drevnejsie v mire chudozestvennye
    kovry I tkani iz oledenelych kurganov Gorgono Altaja*
    (Moscow, 1968)

Rudenko 1970
    Rudenko, Sergei I., tr. M.W. Thompson, *Frozen Tombs
    of Siberia* (Berkeley, 1970), pp. 174–75

Sarre 1923
    Sarre, Friedrich, *Die Kunst des alten Persien* (Berlin, 1923)

Schmidt 1931
    Schmidt, Heinrich, "Seldschukische Seidenstoffe auf
    der Persischen Kunstausstellung in London",
    Belvedere 10 (1931), pp. 81–86

Schorta 2007
    Schorta, Regula, *Dragons of Silk, Flowers of Gold:
    A Group of Liao-Dynasty Textiles at the Abegg-Stiftung*
    (Riggisberg, 2007)

Schulze 1920
    Schulze, Paul, *Alte Stoffe* (Berlin, 1920)

Serjeant 1972
    Serjeant, R. B., *Islamic Textiles: Material for a History
    up to the Mongol Conquest* (Beirut, 1972)

Simpson 1980
    Simpson, Marianna Shreve, *Arab and Persian Painting
    in the Fogg Art Museum* (Cambridge, 1980)

Smirnow 1909
    Smirnow, J. I., *Vostocznoje serebro*
    (St. Petersburg, 1909)

Splendeur Cat. 1993
    *Splendeur des Sassanides: Musées royaux d'Art et
    d'Histoire* (Brussels, 1993) [Exhibition catalogue; no
    named author]

Stauffer 1991
    Stauffer, Annemarie, *Die mittelalterlichen Textilien
    von St. Servatius in Maastricht* (Riggisberg, 1991)

Stein 1928
    Stein, M. A., *Innermost Asia* (Oxford, 1928)

Trever / Lukonin 1987
    Trever, K. V., and V. G. Lukonin, *Sasanidskoe serebro:
    khudozhestvennaya kul'tura Irana III-IV vv. v sobraniyakh
    Gosudarstvennogó Érmitazha* (Moscow, 1987)

Volbach / Kühnel 1926
    Volbach, Wolfgang Fritz, and Ernst Kühnel,
    Late Antique Coptic and Islamic Textiles of Egypt
    (London, 1926)

Wardwell 1987
    Wardwell, Anne E., "Flight of the Phoenix:
    Crosscurrents in Late Thirteenth to Fourteenth-Century
    Silk Patterns and Motifs", *The Bulletin of the Cleveland
    Museum of Art* 74/1 (1987), pp. 2–35

Wardwell 1988–89
    Wardwell, Anne E., "Panni Tartarici: Eastern Islamic
    silks woven with Gold and Silver (13th and 14th
    centuries)", *Islamic Art* 3 (1988–89), pp. 95–173

Wardwell 1989 A
    Wardwell, Anne E., "Recently Discovered Textiles
    Woven in the Western Part of Central Asia before
    A. D. 1220", special issue of *Textile History* 20/2
    (1989), pp. 175–84

Watt / Wardwell 1998
    Watt, James C. Y., and Anne Wardwell,
    *When Silk was Gold: Central Asian and Chinese
    Textiles* (New York, 1997)

Weibel 1952
    Weibel, Adéle Coulin, *Two Thousand Years of Textiles*
    (New York, 1952)

Whitfield / Farrer 1990
    Whitfield, Roderick, and Anne Farrer,
    Caves of the Thousand Buddhas (London, 1990)

Whitfield 1995
    Whitfield, Roderick, *Dunhuang: Die Höhlen der
    klingenden Sande. Buddhistische Kunst an der
    Seidenstraße* (Munich, 1995)

Wieczorek / Lind 2007
    Wieczorek, Alfried, and Christoph Lind (ed.),
    Ursprünge der Seidenstraße (Stuttgart, 2007)

Wilckens 1989
    Wilckens, Leonie von, "Seidengewebe des 12./13.
    Jahrhunderts aus Nordmesopotamien und Bagdad",
    *Jahrbuch des Museums für Kunst und Gewerbe
    Hamburg* 8 (1989), pp. 27–44

Wilckens 1991
    Wilckens, Leonie von, *Die textilen Künste:
    Von der Spätantike bis um 1500* (Munich, 1991)

Villard 1950
    Villard, Ugo Monneret de, *Le Pitture Musulmane al
    Soffitto della Cappella Palatina in Palermo* (Rome, 1950)

Wilckens 1992
    Wilckens, Leonie von, *Mittelalterliche Seidenstoffe
    (Bestandskatalog 18 des Kunstgewerbemuseums)*
    (Berlin, 1992)

Vogelsang-Eastwood 1990
    Vogelsang-Eastwood, Gillian M., *Resist Dyed Textiles
    from Quseir Al-Qadim, Egypt* (Paris, 1990)

Zhao Feng 1999
    Zhao Feng, *Treasures in Silk: An Illustrated History
    of Chinese Textiles* (Hong Kong, 1999)

Zhao Feng 2002
    Zhao Feng (ed.), *Recent Excavations of Textiles in
    China* (Hong Kong, 2002)

Zhao Feng 2007
    Zhao Feng (ed.), *Textiles from Dunhuang in UK
    Collections* (Shanghai, 2007)

TABLE OF CONCORDANCE OF INVENTORY NUMBERS
AND CATALOGUE NUMBERS

Page numbers in *italic* refer to illustrations.

KEY TO TECHNICAL ANALYSIS

S-spin:	ply in anti-clockwise direction
Z-spin:	ply in clockwise direction
V:	number of knots per 10 cm in vertical direction
H:	number of knots per 10 cm in horizontal direction
Z2S:	two Z-spun strands plied together in anti-clockwise direction (S)
Z2:	two Z-spun strands with no discernible ply
Asymmetrical:	asymmetrical or "Persian" knot
Symmetrical:	symmetrical or "Turkish" knot

The number of knots per 10 cm (V and H) can be
used to calculate the number of warps and wefts.
To calculate the knot density per dm², multiply V × H.

Length indicates the warp direction.
Width indicates the weft direction.

INDEX

Figures in *italic* refer to pages on which illustrations appear